MW01076951

"In *Practices*, Roth br
rience under examina
baptism, but also explores less obvious ones, like martyrdom and
radical patience. This book makes a solid addition to the two previous volumes in this series."

—*Brinton L. Rutherford, Lancaster Mennonite Conference*

"In this engaging and thought provoking text, John D. Roth moves
to a core issue for worship: what is the purpose and desired result of
our worship practices? Ultimately, the way we worship impacts the
way we witness to the world regarding the God we worship. Instead
of dwelling on battle lines in the 'worship wars,' Roth moves beyond
issues of form and relevance. He rightly argues that our acts of worship and our witness are inseparable."

—*J. E. McDermond, Messiah College*

"Not just anyone can go into the Christian attic and bring forth 16th-
century treasures that can address critical needs of 21st-century congregations in ways that make a real difference. John Roth is an experienced guide to the Christian past who identifies with the struggles
of contemporary North American Mennonites. In his latest book, he
proves to be a discerning 'scribe of the kingdom.' He knows when to
bring forward the insights of Pilgram Marpeck as well as how to reg-
ister the impact of a beloved hymn in the present. Mennonite readers
will be invited to think about familiar practices in new ways, and they
will be encouraged in their own efforts to rediscover the unity of worship and witness. This book will also be read with appreciation by
Christians from other traditions who struggle to connect worship and
mission with the politics of Jesus. Highly recommended."

—*Michael Cartwright, University of Indianapolis*

"Roth's easy, storytelling writing style, his use of Scripture, and his
insights into the Anabaptist-Mennonite tradition give *Practices* depth

and breadth. The ecumenical conversation links what Anabaptist-Mennonites do with the broader Christian community."

—*Irma Fast Dueck, Canadian Mennonite University*

"John Roth offers a wake-up call—one I hope the church will heed. I resonate deeply with his convictions that the power of the gospel is in the resurrection, that good worship is mission, and that worship is the priority."

—*Marlene Kropf, Mennonite Church USA*

Practices

Also by John D. Roth

Beliefs: Mennonite Faith and Practice
Stories: How Mennonites Came to Be
Engaging Anabaptism: Conversations with a Radical Tradition (editor)

JOHN D. ROTH

Practices

Mennonite Worship
and Witness

Herald Press
Scottdale, Pennsylvania
Waterloo, Ontario

Library of Congress Cataloging-in-Publication Data
Roth, John D., 1960-
  Practices : Mennonite worship and witness / John D. Roth.
    p. cm.
  Includes bibliographical references.
  ISBN 978-0-8361-9427-2 (pbk. : alk. paper)
  1. Mennonites—Liturgy. 2. Anabaptists—Liturgy. 3. Public worship—
Mennonites. 4. Public worship—Anabaptists. 5. Witness bearing (Christianity)—
Mennonites. 6. Witness bearing (Christianity)—Anabaptists. I. Title.
  BX8125.R68 2009
  264'.097—dc22

                                                              2009019608

PRACTICES: MENNONITE WORSHIP AND WITNESS
Copyright © 2009 by Herald Press, Scottdale, Pa. 15683
    Published simultaneously in Canada by Herald Press,
    Waterloo, Ont. N2L 6H7. All rights reserved
International Standard Book Number: 978-0-8361-9427-2
Library of Congress Catalog Card Number: 2009019608
Printed in the United States of America
Cover and book design by Beth Oberholtzer
Cover photo by Wayne Gehman
Sculpture, *The Servant*, by Esther Augsburger

14 13 12 11 10 09   10 9 8 7 6 5 4 3 2 1

To order or request information please call
1-800-245-7894 or visit www.heraldpress.com.

Dedicated to the members of my small group:
Ruth Miller Roth
Dale and Trish Shenk
Peter and Jan Shetler
Andy and Lydia Martin
and their families,
around whose tables I have been fed in body and spirit every week
for more than a decade

Contents

Therefore, in a word, I interpret repentance as regeneration, whose sole end is to restore in us the image of God that had been disfigured and all but obliterated through Adam's transgression. . . . And indeed, this restoration does not take place in one moment or one day or one year; but through continual and even slow advances God wipes out in his elect the corruptions of the flesh, cleanses them of guilt, consecrates them to himself as temples renewing all their minds to true purity that they may practice repentance throughout their lives and know that this warfare will end only at death.

—John Calvin, *Institutes of the Christian Religion,* 3.3.9

Preface

In writing this book I have amassed enormous debts to others. In fact, this is not an original work at all, but really the distillation and recon-figuration—frequently with far less insight, nuance, or originality—of insights borrowed from many other people. Thus readers in the Anabaptist-Mennonite tradition are likely to recognize the debt I owe to people like John Howard Yoder, Stanley Hauerwas, and Marlene Kropf. I also have been very grateful for the wisdom of evangelical Christian authors such as Dallas Willard, Rodney Clapp, Leonard Vander Zee, and Eugene Peterson. And I cannot begin to express my gratitude to Catholic writers like Henri de Lubac, Ronald Rolheiser, and William Cavanaugh. I have benefited enormously from the gifts of the broader Christian church, and I hope that my work might be read in conversation with that broader legacy, even as it is grounded in the his-torical and theological narrative of the Anabaptist-Mennonite tradition I know best and have come to love deeply.

John D. Roth
March 2009

Wrestling with Angels on the Appalachian Trail

Martin Luther, the great leader of the Protestant Reformation in the sixteenth century, once described his work as that of a man climbing the winding staircase of a bell tower in the middle of the night. As he felt his way forward in the dark, his foot slipped, and in desperation he grabbed hold of the only thing he could find—the bell rope. As it turned out, the resolution to Luther's spiritual quandary, which he initially thought was simply a personal matter, rang out loud and clear to many others.

Readers should be quickly assured that I don't pretend to be a latter-day Luther! But the book that follows first came into focus as a result of my own groping in the dark and an effort to seek clarity about questions of faith that seemed quite personal in nature. My hope is that these reflections may speak to questions you may be wrestling with as well.

The circumstances of my spiritual confusion came as something of a surprise. At the time, my life was filled with more blessings than I had reason to deserve. I'd been happily married for twenty-five years. My wife and I had four wonderful children. I was in good health, and I loved my work. But at the same time, I was feeling deeply unsettled. I was at the midpoint of my working career. I had been in the same job for twenty years, and suddenly I was trying to imagine what the next twenty would look like.

The nature of my work was not physically strenuous; yet I often felt tired. For the first time, I began to take note of small aches that lingered, a growing bald spot, and other signs that my body was wearing down. I felt a growing irritability at all the clutter in my life—not just the general busyness, but little things like the growing volume of traffic in my small town, the mounting piles of unsolicited catalogs, and the steady spread of housing developments, golf courses, and strip malls into the fertile cornfields at the edge of town. Even though I had no reason to complain about anything, it seemed that life was becoming increasingly out of focus and fragmented.

Somewhere along the way, Sunday morning worship had begun to feel empty. I sensed that there were people around me who practiced "spiritual disciplines" and were intimate with God. But even though I bought an armful of how-to books on spirituality and Christian growth, my own spiritual life felt brittle and thin. Although I didn't describe it in these words, I know now that I wanted a deeper sense of intimacy with God. I wanted a clearer sense of why the Christian faith that I had espoused for all my adult life was actually "good news" and why I should feel compelled to share that faith with others. In short, I wanted to be "more spiritual."

In retrospect it now seems clear that part of my spiritual unsettledness reflected the larger context of my work. For several years I had been traveling throughout the Mennonite church, speaking to congregations and conferences on a wide range of historical or theological topics. Those travels provided a wonderful opportunity to meet many interesting and creative people who were deeply committed to their congregations, local communities, and the broader church. But along the way, it became clear to me that the church I loved was also struggling to find its way in the midst of deeply uncertain times.

Almost all the congregations I visited clearly desired to be more deliberate in their outreach to the local community and more welcoming to newcomers. Leaders in these churches recognized that for far too long their congregations had existed in a kind of cultural and ethnic isolation from the surrounding communities. Many of these once-thriving churches found themselves in the midst of a slow decline. Young people raised in the congregation were leaving to college and work in other communities. Most of the new members had "married into" the church, where they often struggled to find a home within the well-worn traditions and patterns of the Mennonite faith. In the meantime, newcomers to the area were finding the theology, worship style, or warmth of welcome at other local churches more attractive than what they found among the Mennonites.

In a well-intended effort to break out of these patterns, the congregations I encountered were looking, sometimes desperately, for *spiritual* renewal. Everywhere I went, congregations who had been losing members were hoping to turn things around by experimenting with new forms of worship. Often this meant adopting "progressive" styles of music that included a heavily amplified praise team, PowerPoint projection, and a new repertoire of contemporary Christian music. Some congregations were turning to more liturgical forms of worship, with frequent references to the Common Lectionary and a heavy diet of Taizé songs. Clearly, not everyone was equally enthused about the innovations. But regardless of the style, people seemed to agree that standard forms of Mennonite worship needed to change.

At the same time, many of the congregations I visited also were determined to become more "missional"—more intentional in their outreach to their local communities. But I sensed a deep confusion about what that actually meant. For some congregations, being missional was clearly in tension with everything from their past—historical, cultural, and theological—that would link them to a distinctly Anabaptist or Mennonite identity. Because the cultural trappings of Mennonite ethnicity had been such a barrier to hospitality to newcomers in the past, they reasoned, a missional church would need to downplay (or even consciously reject) denominational distinctives. Traditional Mennonite convictions like pacifism were fine if individuals wanted to embrace them for themselves, but they should never be confused with the gospel. To give these convictions too much emphasis or to make them a test of membership would not only set the bar far too high for new Christians but would also reinforce the traditional image of the Mennonite church as aloof and arrogant.

The Appalachian Trail

Just as these questions and uncertainties were slowly coming into sharper focus, I had the good fortune of being granted a six-month sabbatical from my teaching duties at Goshen College. Initially, I assumed that I would use the sabbatical to do the sort of academic research and writing generally expected of a college professor. But sabbaticals are also occasions for stepping outside the ordinary routines. And one spring morning, I happened to recall a memory from my childhood that gave me a sudden inspiration.

When I was twelve years old, a *National Geographic* arrived in our home that happened to include a large, fan-fold map of the Appalachian Trail, a continuous footpath running 2,174 miles along the eastern United States from Maine to Georgia. For several years, the map hung on the back of my bedroom door, sparking my imagination: wouldn't it be amazing to walk the full width of the United States?

Then, like a lot of childhood treasures, the map disappeared. And gradually the dream of walking the Appalachian Trail receded as the more pressing realities of marriage, parenting, work, and other adult responsibilities came to dominate my life.

Now, however, in the midst of my midlife spiritual discontent, the idea of walking a portion of the Appalachian Trail suddenly reemerged. First it nibbled at the corners of my mind as merely an interesting possibility. Then, as I began to browse websites, read books about the trail, and think about a possible schedule, the idea slowly became an obsession. Hiking the Appalachian Trail was the perfect solution to my spiritual confusion and the deep heaviness I was feeling about the Mennonite church as a whole.

As I understood things at the time, becoming "more spiritual" required a sharp separation from the distractions of other people, the daily routines of ordinary work, and the annoying clutter of email and strip malls. Both Jesus and Paul spent significant periods in solitude in the course of their ministries, and many heroes of the early Christian spiritual tradition were hermits. Time alone, I thought, would bring a new focus to my priorities and open a direct line of communication with God.

I also assumed that being spiritual required discipline, particularly discipline of the body. I knew from plenty of experience how easy it is to yield to the "natural" impulses of the body through overeating, watching sports for hours on end, aimlessly surfing the internet. Attentiveness to the Holy Spirit, by contrast, seemed to require a lot of effort. It did not come naturally but was the reward for those who were able to restrain their impulses, discipline their physical desires, and "win the battle" with their bodily appetites. Walking the Appalachian Trail seemed like an ideal physical endurance test that would force me to become more spiritual.

Finally, it seemed clear to me that a sustained encounter with nature would open fresh opportunities to encounter God. Surely direct communion with God in the beauty of creation would offer a refreshing break from the rituals of Sunday morning worship, which were feeling increasingly dry and mechanical. If my encounters with church institutions and the routines of worship had become drained of life, then communing with nature might open a new path to the divine.

The more I planned, the more significant the trip became in my mind. The hike was no longer a sidebar to the sabbatical. This was to be a vision quest—my chance to wrestle with God alone in the wilderness, to discipline the body, and to commune directly with the divine through nature.

I planned a nineteen-day trip, beginning at the trailhead in Georgia and traveling along the eastern border of Tennessee, through the Smoky Mountains, into North Carolina. It was an ambitious schedule, requiring daily hikes averaging slightly more than twenty miles a day. But the rigor of the plan only added to the challenge. I left Springer Mountain, Georgia, early one morning in late October with exceedingly high hopes.

The trip did not go as planned. On the first day, moving at a brisk pace, I hiked my goal of twenty-three miles before settling into the first campsite. The next day, however, I began to encounter problems. In the morning, I slipped in a stream while filling my water bottle. I changed into dry socks, but as I walked I could feel sores beginning to develop on my softened feet. Not long after that, I misread the map and walked three miles down a mountain before realizing my mistake. Retracing my steps forced me to add six miles to the day's quota. I arrived at my site that evening much later than I had intended, exhausted and almost too tired to eat. I pitched my tent in a clearing at a mountain summit. All night long, I listened to the wind howl. Then I felt the temperature begin to drop, and I woke from a fitful sleep to a cold, drizzling rain.

I got a late start on the third day. That morning it occurred to me that I actually hadn't seen any of the beautiful vistas I had imagined. In fact, most of my attention was focused on the very rocky ground in front of me, picking my way along a trail that followed a monotonous pattern of incline and descent. At noon, I realized I had traveled only seven miles, far from my quota.

By the afternoon, my appetite had disappeared entirely. That night, every joint and muscle in my body ached, and my feet felt shredded. Not once had I pulled out my reading material, much less engaged in deep reflection about the presence of the Holy Spirit or the future of the church. By now the temperature was hovering near freezing.

In the morning of day four, I realized as I put on my socks that blisters had formed on the pads of my feet and several raw sores were emerging between my toes. When I finally got on the trail again, the drizzling rain had turned into sleet, and then snow; a storm spun off by hurricane Wilma in Florida had upset the weather patterns in the region. As a thin glaze of ice formed on the rocks, I began to wonder about the symptoms of hypothermia. Then, numb with cold and exhaustion, I imagined what it would be like to break a leg, there in the wilderness alone at the top of a mountain.

Late in the afternoon, as I crossed a small highway, a pickup truck happened to slow down. When the young driver asked if I needed a ride, I readily climbed in, and he drove me ten miles to the closest town, where I checked in at a budget motel. The following morning, I hitchhiked to the airport in Knoxville, bought a one-way ticket to South Bend, and came home to lick my wounds and to try to make sense of what had just happened.

At one level, I knew that the aborted trip was not such a big deal: the weather was simply bad luck. I should just swallow my pride and try again, this time with more realistic goals. But the truth of the matter was that my sense of confusion and failure went much deeper than that. I had gone to the Appalachian Trail to "become spiritual." I had gone seeking a blessing. I returned home chastened by my failure and feeling more empty than ever.

It is always dangerous to generalize from personal experience. Yet as I have reflected on the spiritual disquietude that led me to the Appalachian Trail—and my deeply misguided attempt to resolve that disquietude—I have been struck by the fact that I am not alone in my confusion.

◆ ◆ ◆

Many Mennonite congregations today are hungry for a more authentic faith, a deeper sense of God's presence in worship, and a clearer understanding of how the gospel matters in daily life. Although the details differ widely, many of those same congregations are tempted, as I was, by the illusion that this spiritual disquietude can be resolved with a fresh technique, an innovative plan, or a new strategic initiative. Church foyers are filled with glossy brochures for leadership training on transformative mission and seminars offering strategies for reaching the unchurched. Church libraries are stocked with books bearing titles like *The Changing Face of Mission, The Seven Habits of a Growing Church,* and *Spirituality for the Busy Believer.*

Countless congregations have struggled to retain their young people by introducing new types of music or jazzing up the sermon with clips from recent movies or retrofitting their buildings with coffee shops and fitness centers, in the hopes that being "relevant" to current cultural tastes will generate an authentic spirituality.

In every instance, the hunger for a more authentic faith and a more relevant witness to the world is real. Our craving for a deeper sense of wholeness, our hunger for God, is genuine. But our inclination to respond to these yearnings with easy "solutions" almost always leaves us disappointed and discouraged.

This book is a sustained reflection on how we might respond to the hunger for God—both individually and collectively—in a more integrated and authentic way. At one level, it seeks to map a deep web of connectedness between abstract terms like *spirituality* and *holiness* and the concrete practices of "Christian ethics." In that sense, it charts a familiar path in the age-old Christian conversation on the relationship between "faith" and "works."

But for reasons I hope will become clear, the real agenda of this book is to convince a Mennonite readership that Christian witness—in its many expressions—always begins with worship. Whether offered to the unchurched in our communities or to hungry refugees in distant parts of the world, the good news of the gospel is authentic and transformative only when it is rooted in a posture of worship. Likewise, the praise we offer God in worship is meaningless—a "resounding gong or a clanging cymbal" (1 Corinthians 13:1)—if it does not find visible, tangible expression in witness. Christian worship and Christian witness are inextricably connected.

The Anabaptists, sixteenth-century forebears of the Mennonites, described this synthesis of worship and witness as "walking in the resurrection of Christ." For them, Christian faith was never understood as a set of abstract theological principles, an inner experience of emotional bliss, or even a "personal relationship" with Jesus. Rather, the life of Christian discipleship begins with our participation in the body of Christ (worship), and it testifies to the power of the resurrection in the world (witness) only when it becomes evident in a transformed way of life (ethics). Cultivating practices that honor the essential unity of worship and witness is at the heart of Christian discipleship and the wellspring of spiritual renewal.

The reflections that follow offer a perspective on the relationship between worship and witness. As will quickly become clear, my understanding of these themes has been deeply shaped by a commitment to the Anabaptist-Mennonite tradition and the struggles of its congregations to embody the Christian faith in their particular settings. But I also hope that the ideas presented here would be recognizable to Christians of all denominational backgrounds.

In the interest of engaging Christians from other traditions in this conversation, it may be helpful to clarify some of my most basic assumptions right from the start.

1. The character of God is revealed in abundance rather than scarcity. In the opening chapter of Genesis we read that God created the world out of *nothing.* In contrast to the persistent human impulse to hoard whatever resources we might have, assuming that creation is finite, God's love and blessing is always excessive, capable of creating something out of nothing. Whether it is manna from heaven so abundant that it cannot be collected (see Exodus 16:21) or the twelve baskets of leftovers after Jesus fed fishes and loaves to five thousand followers (see Mark 6:42-43), God always gives his people what they need—and more!

The gifts of God inevitably exceed our grasp. They spill out beyond our theological definitions; they refuse to be contained within our structures and institutions; they consistently surprise the weak and confound the mighty.

No image captures this central truth more powerfully than that of the Trinity, in which the particular identities of God, Jesus, and the Holy Spirit are joined in unity that exceeds those differences without erasing them. God's abundance is always greater than what we are ever able to imagine or to grasp.

2. The fullest expression of God's revelation to humanity is Jesus Christ, in whom "the Word became flesh" (John 1:14). In this claim we encounter a central paradox of the Christian faith. By definition, God is beyond time, space, and culture. Yet we come to know God *only* within the reality of time, space, and culture. That is, the Holy Spirit is always made known to us in specific, particular, and embodied ways. Although this claim—rooted in the mystery of the incarnation—may seem obvious to most Christians, its implications are profound. For those believers who are used to thinking of God primarily as an emotional feeling or a set of abstract concepts or an invisible spirit, the incarnation reminds us that God comes to humans in bodily form. At the same time, for those believers inclined to think of Jesus primarily as a moral example and wise teacher, the incarnation is a reminder that in Christ we encounter God—the Creator of the universe who is the giver and sustainer of life itself. Because of Jesus, we know that God is present in embodied forms, yet God's presence always exceeds the particularity of the form.

3. Through the Holy Spirit, Christians participate "in Christ" in the life of the church, which we call the body of Christ. Although the resurrected Christ is now seated at the right hand of the Father, he remains present in the church through the gift of the Holy Spirit. As the body of Christ, the church extends the incarnation forward in time and space. In the Gospel of John, Jesus told his disciples "I am the vine; you are the branches. Those who abide in me and I in them bear much fruit" (John 15:5 NRSV). If this living relationship is genuine, Jesus continued, its fruit will be visible in the love that believers demonstrate for each other. Indeed, the love shared among believers in the Christian community—demonstrated in the visible unity of the church—is a powerful witness to the world of the very character of God (see John 17:20-23). This means that salvation can never be defined as a private or personal transaction between an individual believer and God. Rather, we come to know and are transformed by Christ by participating as fruit-bearing members in the church—the body of Christ made visible in the world.

4. The body of Christ is given for the world in acts of vulnerable and self-giving love. This audacious claim seems to fly in the face of common sense. The Creator of the universe voluntarily entered into the flow of human history in the form of a baby, born to poor parents in a backwater province of the Roman Empire. He preached and modeled a life of service to others—especially to those who were weak and vulnerable—and seemingly ended his career by dying a painful and humiliating death on the cross.

Yet it was precisely this vulnerable act of self-giving love that revealed the true nature of God's power and authority. Death could not defeat the power of love. In the resurrection, Christ emerged victorious and invites us to participate in this "power made . . . perfect in weakness" (2 Corinthians 12:9). In his letter to the church at Philippi, Paul summarized this point with poetic clarity. "If you have any encouragement from being united with Christ," Paul wrote, then be

> like-minded [with Christ], having the same love, being one in spirit and purpose. Do nothing out of selfish ambition or vain conceit, but in humility consider others better than yourselves. Each of you should look not only to your own interests, but also to the interests of others.
>
> Your attitude should be the same as that of Christ Jesus: Who, being in very nature God, did not consider equality with God something to be grasped, but made himself nothing, taking the very nature of a servant, being made in human likeness. And being found in appearance as a man, he humbled himself and became obedient to death—even death on a cross! Therefore God exalted him to the highest place and gave him the name that is above every name, that at the name of Jesus every knee should bow, in heaven and on earth and under the earth, and every tongue confess that Jesus Christ is Lord, to the glory of God the Father. (Philippians 2:2-11)

This is the character of God and the secret of God's gift to the world. Accepting this gift means that we too can let go of our desire for earthly power and glory, and be raised up in a new kind of power, one rooted in the confession of Jesus as Lord and expressed in praise, "to the glory of God the Father."

*5. In Christian "practices," worship and witness become insepara-
ble.* Although the term *practices* is not found in Scripture, it captures
a crucial element of the faith that is central to biblical Christianity.
Later chapters will develop the concept of practices in more detail. For
the moment, it may be enough to note that Christian practices are
attitudes and actions—consciously nurtured in the context of the
church and infused by the presence of the Holy Spirit—that make
Christ's presence visible to the world. The regular practices of worship
help to reveal the true nature of reality: all things, both spiritual and
material, are ultimately united in Christ.

Since God's glory is always revealed in physical, tangible, material
ways, worship inevitably finds expression in visible forms: the Word
was made flesh. Thus the distinction that we so often make between
personal piety and ethics, or between inner peace with God and our
witness to peace in the world, no longer makes sense. Practices of worship prepare Christians to "bear witness" to Christ in every aspect of
our daily lives: in our physical bodies, in our families, in our relations
with other members of the church, in our communities, and in the
way we treat God's creation. In this sense, all of the Christian life is an
expression of worship; all of the Christian life is a witness to the Word
made flesh.

Each of these themes, of course, begs for greater clarification,
firmer grounding in Scripture, and more careful nuance. I trust
that this will happen in the chapters that follow.

Part 1 focuses on worship but begins by considering the source of
our dissatisfaction. Chapter 1 explores the deeper roots behind the spiritual disquietude that drove me to the Appalachian Trail and has fos-
tered the confusion evident in many Mennonite congregations in
North America regarding worship and witness. Hidden beneath the
daily routines of life, powerful and disruptive forces are driving a wedge
between God and humanity and fostering an unhealthy division
between our spirit and our body, between the church and the world,
and between our worship and our witness. Identifying the sources of
our spiritual malaise is a first step toward addressing the deep causes of
our disease rather than merely treating the visible symptoms.

Chapters 2, 3, and 4 suggest a path toward healing. Chapter 2 outlines the foundational significance of the incarnation for every aspect of Christian faith and practice and recalls the reasons Christians throughout history have regularly gathered for worship. The incarnation—the Word made flesh in the person of Jesus Christ—is the key to healing the deep divisions that separate us from each other, from the created world, and above all from God. In worship, the focus of chapter 3, we celebrate the incarnation by recalling, and entering into, the story of God's saving acts in history. True worship will inevitably spill out into the world in the visible form of transformed lives: worship is inherently missional. Chapter 4 introduces the concept of *practices* as a defining characteristic of the Christian life. Practices of worship nurture in us the distinctive habits and dispositions that characterize a Christian way of living in the world. Christian practices are a form of witness; they make the body of Christ visible to the world.

Part 2 examines how worship is embodied in the witness of our daily lives. Chapter 5 explores the relationship between worship and our physical bodies, focusing especially on such themes as singing, foot washing, shared meals, and dying well. Chapter 6 examines worship practices that are expressed in family life, with special attention to marriage, child rearing, mutual aid, and forgiveness. Chapter 7 traces the links between Christian worship and the church's witness in our communities and the world, while Chapter 8 considers the physical places and spaces of worship, noting some ways church architecture shapes our worship while also communicating many of our deepest values.

Finally, Part 3 reflects on the future of Mennonite worship and witness. Chapter 9 offers an Anabaptist-Mennonite perspective on the practices of baptism and communion—rituals that reenact the incarnation and help Christians to "re-member," or reconstitute, themselves as the living body of Christ. Chapter 10 considers why worship and witness must ultimately be rooted in beauty. In the end, I suggest, the most powerful form of mission is not a carefully worded testimony or even an example of moral perfection; rather, it is a consistent way of being in the world that bears witness to "the beauty of holiness."

◆ ◆ ◆

A final word about method may be appropriate. I realize that some readers may find the central argument of this book—that worship is inseparable from the embodied practices of Christian witness—to be an exercise in circular logic. Wouldn't it make more sense to consider worship and witness as two separate and distinct activities? Worship is what we do for two hours on Sunday morning; witness is the task at hand for the rest of the week. Or worship has to do with the private inner life of the believer while witness is a public expression of our shared faith. Or worship is the time when we are "energized" to go back out into the world to do the hard work of living virtuously.

These are indeed tempting options, especially because these distinctions seem so deeply entrenched. In the Mennonite church today, this is perhaps nowhere more visible than in the meaning of the word *peace*. In the current caricatures of our time, Mennonite congregations face one of two choices: they can either be committed to an inner "peace with God," usually associated with expressive forms of worship and a welcoming embrace of popular culture; or they can focus on "peace and justice," which usually implies an outward emphasis on service, concern for the earth, political activism, and a critical view of popular culture. Both groups use the word *peace* but in ways that seem to keep worship and witness in distinct—even hostile—categories.

In this book I want to consciously resist the temptation to separate worship and witness. On the one hand, these distinctions almost always have the effect of reducing worship to a technique or exercise designed to produce a specific outcome—usually to make us feel happy or peaceful or energized for the week ahead. Yet biblical worship is never understood as a means to an end. Instead, worship is nothing more (or less!) than consciously adopting the appropriate posture of humans beings to their Creator, which is one of adoration and praise. Worship is its own reward.

Nonetheless, because we have been saved by a God who visited the earth in human form, our salvation inevitably will take on a visible expression in the form of transformed lives: worship always leads to witness.

By the same token, I generally describe the embodied or enacted practices of Christians—the things Christians do—in the language of witness rather than in the more traditional terminology of "ethics." Living a life of Christian virtue, as I understand it, is not primarily a matter of being a good person or devising strategies for making peace or being a vigilant defender of justice, though none of these things are inherently bad. Christian ethics make sense—they are a true expression of witness in the world—only to the extent that our actions emerge out of our participation in the body of Christ. Like worship, witness is not primarily about us! It is simply the inevitable result of human beings living in appropriate relation to their Creator. Christian witness in the world is nothing more (or less!) than the presence of the Spirit taking on visible form in our lives. It is not, as Paul writes, I who live, "but Christ lives in me" (Galatians 2:20). Thus worship is always a public activity that transforms our actions; and our actions are always a public witness to the God whom we worship.

In the end, however, this understanding of faith is not an argument to be won or lost. It is not a mathematical formula to be demonstrated with an airtight proof. The Christian faith is an invitation, not a threat; a witness to be borne, not a demand to be imposed. Its authority is ultimately anchored in nothing more than the testimony and practices of the living body of Christ.

When all is said and done, the appeal of the Christian faith rests on this simple invitation: taste and see that the Lord is good!

Part 1

Worship

1

A Divided Life

Exiles from Eden

> *By the rivers of Babylon we sat down and wept when we remembered Zion; there on the poplars we hung our harps, for there our captors asked us for songs, our tormentors demanded songs of joy. . . . How can we sing the songs of the Lord while in a foreign land?*
>
> —PSALM 137:1-4

In January of 2002, when Cardinal Bernard Law of Boston publicly acknowledged that several priests in his jurisdiction had sexually abused children, we might have expected news of the scandal, however painful, to quickly fade from national attention. After all, any institution as large as the Catholic Church is likely to have a few individuals who fail to live up to the standards. But the problem refused to go away. As it turned out, what happened in Boston was hardly an isolated incident. In the months that followed, scores of individuals in major cities across the United States came forward with similar stories of childhood abuse at the hands of those whom they had trusted and regarded as the human face of the church.

Even worse was the evidence of the church's complicity in the problem: in diocese after diocese, bishops had "resolved the problem" by simply reassigning priests accused of sexual abuse to new parishes. Five years after Cardinal Law's public statement, the church found itself embroiled in lawsuits involving thousands of people in dioceses from New York to Los Angeles that resulted in settlements totaling more than a billion dollars. Untangling the legal issues may take decades. But the pain—both individual and collective—will not be resolved by court settlements or financial payouts. Although the church has worked hard to address the problems, its public image in the United States has been unquestionably tarnished.

Lest Protestants start to feel smug, however, stories of moral failure in the church are certainly not limited to Catholics. In recent decades, dozens of prominent Protestant preachers—many with staunchly conservative positions on issues of morality, family values, and personal integrity—have been brought to public shame for their ethical shortcomings. For many critics, this blatant hypocrisy only confirmed their skepticism about celebrity pastors who seem more focused on a gospel of personal wealth than on compassion for the poor.

It would be nice to say that these problems in the church—this gap between professed belief and actual practice—was limited to a few visible leaders, the unfortunate result of too much power, fame, and money. Unfortunately, the church's struggle for public credibility goes deeper than this. In his 2005 book, *The Scandal of the Evangelical Conscience*, evangelical activist Ron Sider argues that professing Christians from all walks of life—every culture and race, the rich and poor, the educated and uneducated—find themselves struggling to live with integrity. In 2001, for example, the divorce rate among born-again Christians was exactly the same as that of the general American population, with 90 percent of these divorces occurring after the couple had accepted Christ. Husbands who identify themselves as "theologically conservative" commit domestic abuse at least as often as men in the general public. Evangelical Christians are among the groups most likely to object to a black family moving into their neighborhood. In 2002, only 6 percent of born-again Christians tithed 10 percent or more of their incomes; overall, evangelicals contribute about 4 percent of their income to the church. According to numerous public opinion polls, people outside the church generally perceive Christians as mean-spirited, oppressive to women, narrow in their political agen-

da, dismissive of other religions, and dogmatically literal in their interpretation of the Bible.

These gloomy statistics are reinforced by larger trends in
American churches. According to several recent surveys, worship
attendance in the six mainline Protestant denominations declined
between 1994 and 2005 in real numbers by some 12 percent. In
recent years, virtually all Christian denominations have faced significant budget reductions, with declining dollars available for missions, publications, education, and administration. At the same time,
young people are far less likely than they were a generation ago to
commit themselves to the Christian faith; increasingly, eighteen- to
thirty-year-olds are inclined to say that they are "spiritual, but not
religious" or that they "believe in God, but not the church."

And the bad news hits even closer to home. For generations,
groups in the Anabaptist-Mennonite tradition have liked to describe
themselves as "a people apart"—a people "nonconformed" to the
dominant currents shaping the broader culture. That assumption, if
it ever was true, no longer holds. A recent study of Mennonite Church
USA suggests that the denomination, like virtually every other, is
struggling to cope with an aging membership, shrinking budgets,
waning allegiance to church traditions, and a blurred theological
identity. Between 1989 and 2005, Mennonite Church USA experienced a 16-percent decline in membership, while the average age of
members increased from forty-nine to fifty-four. Less than one-third
of those surveyed claimed to have a "very strong commitment" to the
denomination; one-third have never invited a non-Christian to attend
a service or activity at their church; and only 51 percent speak about
their faith to persons outside of church or family at least once a month.

In reading through this litany of woe, our first impulse is to
react defensively. These trends may be true of some Christians, we
are tempted to say, but they do not describe me or my church.

Such reactions are understandable. Yet the concerns at stake here
go deeper than the worrisome statistics of survey data. Ask any
Christian on the street about his or her moral convictions, and no one
is likely to celebrate greed, praise racism, encourage sexual infidelity,

or argue that divorce is a good thing. The problem is not that we have lost sight of the ideal. The deeper issue is our persistent inability to bring our professed beliefs into alignment with our practices and the problem this poses for our public witness.

Once we get beyond our defensiveness, we are still confronted with these questions: Why does the Christian church have such a significant credibility problem? Why are young people not inclined to regard the church as worthy of their time and creative energy? Why is our witness to the world so often compromised by the failure of our practice? Why is it that our desire to do the right thing—to spend more time with our family; to share the good news of the gospel with a co-worker; to volunteer at the local literacy program; to pass by the pornography sites; to pursue a healthier diet—consistently gets pushed aside by the pressures of the moment? How is it that Christians who are absolutely clear about doctrine, who enjoy a regular diet of biblically grounded sermons, and who lift their hands in praise to inspiring Christian music can be swept along the rest of the week by the deep currents of our culture?

The Water in Which We Are Swimming

These are not new questions, of course. From the very beginning of the church at Pentecost, Christians have always struggled to bring their lives into conformity with the teachings of Jesus. The epistles to the young churches in the New Testament are filled with strong language against immoral behavior and inappropriate practices that apparently had crept into those congregations. Paul himself expressed deep frustration at the persistent gap between his own ideals and his actual practice (see Romans 7:14-25). Later, church theologians like Augustine reflected at great length on the stubborn grip that sin seems to have on the human will, even for those who have committed themselves to the church.

What seems clear in these writings is that the struggle to bring our practice into conformity with our stated beliefs runs much deeper than our intentions. Teachings that seem so clear in a sermon or in Scripture suddenly become considerably more complicated when we try to apply them to the messy realities of daily life. We know, for example, that Jesus instructed his followers to be generous with their possessions: "Give to everyone who asks you," he taught (Luke 6:30). And we might honestly want to do as Jesus commanded. But the moment we try to put this teaching into practice, we immediately run into a series of personal and practical questions that seem to make this simple teaching considerably more complicated.

Throughout the history of the church, Christians in various traditions have attempted to resolve this gap between teaching and practice in a variety of ways. The Catholic Church tended to accept a division between those who were called to the "counsels of perfection"—the clergy and especially those living in monastic orders—and the majority of laypeople, who were not expected to follow the teachings of Jesus with the same sort of rigor or consistency. Some Protestant traditions have insisted that Christ's teachings were intended to focus our attention on a future kingdom of God: they alert us to the perfection of heaven but were never intended as literal expectations for Christians who are still living in a fallen world. Others have argued that it is precisely our inability to live up to the commandments of Christ (law) that keeps us focused on the fact that salvation is a pure, unmerited gift of God's forgiveness (grace). Christians who profess Christ as Lord are still sinners, but they are sinners who know that God forgives them nonetheless.

The Anabaptist-Mennonite tradition has framed these tensions somewhat differently. The crucial distinction is not the one separating laity and clergy, or between the current age and a future kingdom of God, or even between law and grace. Rather, the line that matters most is the one dividing the church (the body of Christ) from the larger culture that has not yet acknowledged Christ's lordship (the "world"). Mennonites have traditionally quoted Paul's admonition to the church "Do not be conformed to the pattern of this world" (Romans 12:2). As a consequence Mennonites historically have tended to define themselves over against the world, often by the things they did *not* do:

Mennonites did not serve in the military; did not wear jewelry; did not dance, go to movies, drink, or smoke.

Yet this apparent clarity regarding the boundaries between the church and the broader culture turns out to be something of an illusion. Like everyone else, Mennonites are deeply embedded in culture: after all, they speak a language, they have jobs, they carry passports, they live in communities, and they express their faith in ways that reflect the very culture they are critiquing. Despite a theological tradition that has often been suspicious of culture, Mennonites—like all Christians—are always immersed in a particular cultural context.

What makes this so challenging for Christian discernment is that our culture often presents itself to us as inevitable—as the "way things really are"—so that it becomes difficult to recognize aspects of culture that may need to be critiqued or transformed. A swimmer trying to cross the English Channel with the tide running out to sea may not be aware that even as he is swimming toward the opposite shore, the currents are moving him in a direction that is almost impossible to discern. Such is the nature of culture. It is the water in which we are swimming. We are often so focused on the surface ripples—and the mere challenge of staying afloat—that we lose sight of the deeper currents moving us in a direction we did not intend and can only barely perceive. The challenge for Christians is not to pretend they can swim without getting wet; it is rather to keep their eyes focused on Christ and to be mindful of these deep currents, which can easily sweep us off course if we fail to be attentive.

Being Mindful of the Currents: The Nature of Modern Culture

Generalizations about culture are always risky. Our lives are shaped by so many variables—ethnicity, income, geography, religion—that any assertions about modern culture are bound to be incomplete. Nonetheless, people living in most western cultures today would almost certainly recognize several common characteristics. The following themes, I suggest, are among the deep currents shaping our lives to which Christians should be particularly attentive.

1. An individualistic culture. Since the European Enlightenment of the eighteenth century, much of western political culture has been devoted to defining, preserving, and extending individual rights. Most of us take it for granted that all people should be free to define themselves however they wish, independent of inherited traditions, family reputation, or religious identity. As long as you do not infringe on other people's freedoms, you should be able to do whatever you want to do, become whoever you want to become, and shape your identity in whatever way you please.

At one level, of course, Christians celebrate the unique personality and character of every individual. God created us as distinct persons, each with unique gifts, insights, and personality. But for many people today, the quest for freedom—particularly the freedom from external limits or constraints on our choices—has elevated individualism and the right to define our own identity as the primary measure of the good life. An individualistic culture places a higher value on rights and liberties than it does on responsibilities or obligations. Cultures committed to individualism have a limited vocabulary for talking about the common good or the virtues of humility and patience. Formal commitments in a culture preoccupied with individual liberty—to my spouse or family, to the church, to tradition—will likely not be binding but strategic (do they help me further my goals?) and temporary (do they restrict my freedoms?). In ways that we scarcely recognize, we are taught to regard any restrictions on our choices as inherently oppressive.

2. A fragmented culture. One extension of individualism in our culture is the freedom it offers to make innumerable choices. Think, for example, of the hundreds of television channels now at our fingertips or the way in which the internet allows us to "surf" randomly through a nearly infinite number of websites. But even as we celebrate the remarkable variety of choices at our disposal, we also are vaguely aware that our lives are becoming increasingly fragmented and compartmentalized.

In a single day, many of us move rapidly from one context to another, almost as if we were switching channels on TV, instantly adjusting to the assumptions of each new setting. We routinely multi-task at our jobs—planning dentist appointments, scheduling plumbers, making dinner reservations, even as we move from one project or conversation or committee meeting to the next. Friendships at work or in our recreational pursuits rarely overlap with our relationships at church. We live in neighborhoods where we regularly encounter numerous cultures and languages. We are members of professional societies, unions, time-share clubs, community groups, sports teams, and church committees. Dozens of different magazines—many of them unsolicited—arrive each week in our mailbox. Our email accounts are bombarded with spam. Advertising images flash constantly across our mind. All of this means that our lives are rich with color and variety. But it also suggests a fragmentation of life into many discrete parts in which our roles and identities instantly shift as we move from one setting to the next.

For the Christian, the fragmentation of our culture raises the question as to whether the church is anything more than merely one more special-interest group competing for our time and attention. In the midst of this kaleidoscope of options, what would it mean for the Christian to have a coherent worldview or a consistent ethic or an identity that extends beyond our worship service on Sunday morning into the blurry demands of life the rest of the week?

3. A mass culture. Even as we celebrate our individualism and the overwhelming variety of choices in modern culture, we are also dimly aware that our lives are profoundly influenced by large-scale forces almost beyond our comprehension or control. For example, virtually all our news and entertainment comes from what we call the mass media. The television and movie industries (to say nothing of politics) invest enormous resources in testing markets to make sure their offerings will have mass appeal. Many of our consumer choices are shaped by global corporations that pay millions of advertising dollars for a share of our pocketbooks. Most of us simply assume that things like interstate highways, consolidated schools, shopping malls, and mail-order catalogs are an inevitable part of modern life.

Mass culture has certainly helped to make the world smaller. And it has given us more consumer choices, often at prices that working people can afford. But there are also some real costs. Mass-produced consumer goods often require people to work long hours for low pay, and may ultimately lead to the loss of local skills and handcrafts.

We sometimes talk enthusiastically about the "global village"—how modern communication allows people all over the world to be in instant conversation with each other. But in a mass culture, the language of *village* is misleading. Villagers, after all, truly know each other, including the particular gifts and eccentric habits of each individual. Villagers share memories that extend over generations. If mass culture honors efficiency and technical skills, village culture honors relationships and wisdom. The difference is significant. For Christians, living in a mass culture raises profound questions about what it means to truly know each other and what would it mean to be truly known.

4. An instant culture. Yet another characteristic of modern culture is the high value it places on speed. Indeed, we generally assume that anything done faster must be better. Thus bookstores offer entire shelves of new publications devoted to instant diets, get-rich-quick strategies, and promises of spiritual growth in one-minute-a-day lessons. Popular TV shows demonstrate how to "makeover" your body or your house in the flicker of an eye. Round-the-clock news outlets distill complex world events into breaking "headline news," and political pundits offer solutions to the crises of our day with a few bullet points. Our food industry has been transformed around the promise of convenience and speed, so that we do not think twice about the merits of "fast food" or the benefits of instant potatoes, microwave popcorn, prepackaged cookie dough, and boneless chicken. We have been conditioned to expect computers to operate instantaneously—at "twitch speed"—so that any delay of more than a millisecond generates a burst of impatience within us.

Greater efficiencies can free up more time for other aspects of life, of course. But as the overall pace of our culture speeds up, so do our expectations. Instead of celebrating the additional time granted us, we are more likely to become increasingly anxious about all the experiences we may be missing. Somewhere in our minds we know that the things that really matter in life—like raising children, developing committed relationships, building a community of friends—require time, consistency, patient nurturing, discipline, and attentiveness. But our cultural obsession with speed tempts us to look for shortcuts and quick solutions whenever we can.

5. A culture of consumption. As with every other aspect of modern culture, there is nothing intrinsically wrong with producing or consuming. Making things, after all, is a form of creativity that reflects the very character of God, and the fruits of our labors can be part of the goodness of creation. But Christians should take note of how explicitly the logic of production and consumption appeals to our sinful natures and how easily these impulses can become idolatrous. Notice, for example, how often our economic system today is described in language once reserved for God:

- Like God, the market is *omnipresent*—it's everywhere. There's no escaping it. On average we are exposed to more than three thousand advertisements every day, each appealing to our desires rather than our needs.
- Like God, the market is *omniscient*—it's all-knowing. If we just leave our hands off of it and allow competition to play itself out, the argument goes, everyone will benefit.
- And like God, the market is *omnipotent*—it's all-powerful. Appeals to its logic—the bottom line of costs and profits—is the last word. If the deal is a moneymaker, all other considerations fall away.

The impact of a consumer culture has shaped us in profound ways. During the first decade of the twentieth century, 40 percent of Americans spent more than they earned. The average credit-card debt in 2008 was nearly eight thousand dollars. One of the fastest-growing small businesses in recent years is storage rental facilities: we simply own too much stuff to fit it into our expanding homes. Along the way we begin to confuse happiness with the adrenaline rush of shopping, and we unconsciously begin to define relationships in terms of risks, costs, and profits.

This, in very broad strokes, is the nature of the currents in which we are swimming. We live in an individualistic culture, a fragmented culture, a mass culture, an instant culture, and a culture that defines us in market terms.

And it's not all bad! By almost all the standard measures, Christians in North America have richly benefited from the political, economic, and cultural opportunities of western society. But with the benefits have also come some genuine costs. The freedom to travel and the pursuit of job opportunities have made our world small indeed. Yet our constant mobility has also left us feeling adrift—cut off from a sense of place or home and disoriented by the blur of constantly shifting landscapes.

Modern advertising experts have been quick to recognize our rootless condition and to offer us substitutes: Cracker Barrel's illusion of a small-town country store, for example, or Kentucky Fried Chicken's promise to make us a meal that tastes just like Grandma's. Deep down, however, we know that these are artificial contrivances, far from the real thing, even though they may provide temporary comfort.

Our culture has given us an enormous range of opportunities. Yet we sometimes find ourselves living empty lives. We have an infinite number of choices, but still feel lonely and cut off.

At the heart of all these anxieties—at the core of our alienation from each other and from ourselves—is a dim awareness that we are separated from our Creator. Behind our hunger for wholeness is a desire for God. Augustine's prayer summarized it eloquently: "Our hearts are restless until they find rest in you."

Exiles in the Promised Land

Psalm 137, quoted at the beginning of this chapter, uses the language of exile to capture the sense of alienation I have been describing. Like many Christians in North America, the children of Israel had understood themselves to be a people with a special purpose and mission. They had a wonderful tradition rooted in God's covenant with Abraham and Sarah, the dramatic account of the exodus out of slavery in Egypt, and the mighty acts of God that led them into the Promised Land, where they had become a great nation united around the city of Jerusalem.

But then disaster struck. First the Assyrians attacked and destroyed the ten northern tribes of Israel. Then the Babylonians defeated the remaining two tribes, demolished the walls of Jerusalem, and carted the survivors off to exile in a distant and foreign land. Cut off from their homeland, their history, and each other, the exiles began to wonder whether God had forgotten them. How, the psalmist asked, could they possibly sing the Lord's song in this strange culture? Where can refugees find good news?

Christians in North America today are certainly not refugees in the same sense as their Christian brothers and sister in the Sudan or Congo who have literally lost their homes. But exile can be a spiritual as well as a physical reality. And many Mennonites today do feel a sense of exile. Familiar cultural patterns that once provided a sense of "peoplehood" no longer seem sustainable. The tight web of social and economic relationships—nurtured by an agrarian lifestyle and geographic proximity—are now fading memories. A tradition that once provided Mennonite young people with a sense of identity and place no longer seems attractive. And, at an even deeper level, faith itself can seem like a psychological trick or a crutch for the weak or unstable.

In the face of our deep hunger for assurance, connection, and coherence, it sometimes seems that the church itself is being swept along by the deep currents of our culture. Increasingly, for example, the language and practices of Christianity reinforces, rather than challenges, the individualism of our day. So much of the vocabulary of contemporary religion is focused on personal piety or on a private prayer life or on how the church can "get me where I want to go." We have a growing fascination with large-scale Christianity. We are impressed with the strategies of TV ministries and megachurch operations designed for mass appeal; we are attracted to glossy brochures about seminars in church growth that promise to increase our numbers. We are hungry for quick results, willing to measure church growth primarily in terms of the number of people in our pews. Along the way, we are becoming religious consumers, talking without much shame about "church shopping" and about finding a congregation suited to our needs.

We hope that these solutions will resolve the challenges we face. Yet we often fail to recognize how the solutions to the church's challenges end up mirroring the culture it is trying to resist. In the end, what we really seem to have in mind is not a living, breathing congregation but something more like Wal-Mart: a full range of choices with lots of self-serve express lanes and all at the cheapest possible price. Like people drinking salt water, our efforts to assuage our thirst ultimately leave us craving more.

This description may strike some as exaggerated in its pessimism. But before we can talk enthusiastically about the way forward, we dare not avoid the first step of taking a serious look at our current condition. The church is hungry for renewal. Yet if we are to bridge the gap between who we are and who we want to be, the bridge must start and end on firm foundations rather than wishful thinking. And the bridge itself must be strong enough to bear the load, which means that solutions appealing primarily to the emotions or to abstract ideals are not going to be helpful, nor are reforms based on quick-fix strategies or grit-your-teeth-determination.

Is There Any Hope for Exiles?

The good news for the church always begins with a reminder of God's faithfulness and abundance: God never abandons the church, and

God always gives us all we need to worship him and to be faithful witnesses.

Clues to the way forward might be found in the words of the Lord's Prayer, a prayer so familiar that we often overlook its revolutionary claims. The prayer begins with an expression of worship ("hallowed by thy name") and moves immediately into a remarkable petition. When Christians pray "thy kingdom come, thy will be done; on earth as it is in heaven," we are making an astounding request. In that phrase we are asking God to heal the divisions that separate us from God's intended purpose: we are asking that our life on earth be fully reconciled with the kingdom of God in heaven. The prayer goes on to acknowledge our dependence on God for our most basic material needs ("give us this day our daily bread") and spiritual needs ("forgive us our sins, as we forgive those who sin against us"), before concluding with another full-throated expression of worship ("for thine is the kingdom and the power and the glory, for ever and ever. Amen").

The reflections that follow assume that all of the crucial elements of the Christian faith can be found in this prayer. Christian faith begins and ends with worship; everything else is an expression of our longing for God's presence to be realized fully here and now, in time and space, in our daily lives. This hope has animated the Anabaptist-Mennonite tradition from its beginnings in the sixteenth century. The Anabaptists—and their descendent groups like the Mennonites, Amish, and Hutterites—insisted that Christians who prayed the Lord's Prayer would be empowered by the Holy Spirit to follow Christ in deed as well as word, in action as well as intention, with their hands as much as their heads or hearts.

"No one can truly know Christ," the Anabaptist preacher Hans Denck famously argued, "unless he follows after him in life." Throughout our history, we have consistently fallen short of that ideal. But that conviction has remained clear nonetheless. It is a hope grounded in God's abundance, an abundance made real to us only to the extent that we offer it as good news for the world; a hope rooted in Jesus' ministry of reconciliation, which empowers us to participate with God in the healing of a broken and divided world.

2

An Undivided Life

Why the Incarnation Matters

He is the image of the invisible God, the firstborn over all creation. . . . He is before all things, and in him all things hold together. And he is the head of the body, the church; he is the beginning and the firstborn among the dead, so that in everything he might have the supremacy. For God was pleased to have all fullness dwell in him, and through him to reconcile to himself all things, whether things on earth or things in heaven, by making peace through his blood, shed on the cross.

—COLOSSIANS 1:15, 18-20

On the ceiling of the Sistine Chapel in Rome—the center around which Michelangelo's stunning portrayal of biblical history revolves—is a painting known as "The Creation of Adam." On one side of the painting we see an image of God, a majestic yet kindly figure with a flowing white beard, stretching out the index finger of his right hand. On the opposite side is the reclining figure of Adam. As Michelangelo envisioned this dramatic moment in the creation story, God is clearly initiating the action: his body seems to be straining toward Adam, taking up a full two-thirds of the scene.

Adam, by contrast, is relaxing comfortably on the ground. Although he extends his left hand toward the finger of God, the gesture seems tentative, almost indifferent. The focal point of the image, barely visible to the viewers below, is the tension-filled space that remains between God's outstretched finger and Adam's hesitant response. Clearly, if the fingers are going to touch, it is Adam who will need to make the move.

Michelangelo's painting captures the essence of a question that humans have pondered since the beginning of time: how do heaven and earth meet? How does the transcendent world of the Spirit intersect with the material world of time and space? How are humans reconciled with God?

For Christians, the answer is both profoundly simple and remarkably complex. Heaven and earth meet—humans are reconciled with God—in the person of Jesus Christ. Jesus bridges the gap between God and humans. In the language of Christian theology, Jesus is God incarnate—"in the flesh."

This is a stunning claim! Jesus is not "a god" or "a metaphor for God" or "a lot like God." No, Jesus *is* God in human form. In the flesh-and-blood body of Jesus, God has become one with humanity. "In the beginning," writes the apostle John in the opening of his Gospel, "was the Word, and the Word was with God, and the Word was God. . . . The Word [referring here to Jesus] became flesh" (John 1:1, 14). "Anyone who has seen me," Jesus tells his astonished disciples, "has seen the Father" (John 14:9). For those who still had doubts, Jesus sometimes came straight to the point: "I and the Father are one" (John 10:30).

The Christian tradition has struggled mightily for words, images, and concepts adequate to communicate this astounding paradox. Early on, the church fathers invented language like *the Trinity*, the *virgin birth*, and the *incarnation* to help explain this seemingly incomprehensible mystery. Along the way, other theologians have tried to distinguish between the "earthly" and the "glorified" flesh of Jesus. They have introduced precise phrases such as "begotten of the Father, not created." They have engaged in strenuous debates over words like *essence* and *modalism* and even came close to dividing the church over the question of whether Jesus was "of the same substance" as God (*homoousis*) or of a "similar substance" as God (*homoiousis*).

Though some modern people are inclined to look on this as pointless theological hairsplitting, the issues at stake in these debates have real consequences. If Christian conversion and transformation is more than merely a psychological fantasy, just how do sinful, finite, limited humans become holy? If the church—limited as it is in time, space, and culture—is more than merely another social institution, how does it become the living body of Christ or the kingdom of God? In short, how does the Word become flesh?

In Chapter 1, we explored various ways in which deep currents in our culture often leave us feeling isolated, empty, and alone. The true source of that loneliness, I suggested, is a spiritual, rather than a cultural, problem. At the heart of our yearning for wholeness is the fact that we are separated from God, from each other, and from creation itself. We ended with a fundamental question: how can the unity of spirit and body—the harmony, intimacy, and wholeness—that God intended for us in creation be restored? How can heaven and earth be joined together again?

This chapter will not provide a full answer to these questions. But for anyone who feels sometimes as if you are in exile—at war with your body, at odds with your spouse or neighbor, alienated from creation, and distant from God—a deeper understanding of the incarnation may offer a useful road map for finding your way home.

How Do Heaven and Earth Meet?

When Christians talk about the incarnation (literally, "enfleshment"), they usually are referring to Jesus Christ—God's unique revelation to the world in human form. Yet hints of the incarnation are evident throughout the entire biblical story, beginning with the opening chapters of the biblical story of creation.

The book of Genesis describes a universe that God has called into existence out of nothing. In the biblical language, God's Spirit "moved on the face of the deep" and the universe began to take on an ordered form. Creation would not exist without God's initiative, and each ordered step—light separated from darkness, sky from water, earth from the oceans—reveals God's presence in the material world. Creation itself is filled with spirit of God!

In the culminating act of creation, God shaped a human form out of clay. In the flesh and blood of our physical bodies, humans are undeniably joined to the earth. But that form, according to Genesis, was also shaped "in the image of God" (1:27; 9:6). And it became fully human only when God breathed into our nostrils the breath of life— a gift of a living spirit that is absolutely essential to our humanity.

So we are both flesh *and* spirit, both body *and* soul: the two cannot be divided. It was precisely this fusion of the created material world with the breath of God's Spirit that God pronounced to be good.

God created us as incarnated beings—ensouled bodies, embodied souls. And God called it good!

The creation story in the first three chapters of Genesis also suggests that part of the goodness of creation was God's intention for humans to live in complete trust and intimacy and harmony—not only with God, but also with each other and with nature itself. Yet, as we know all too well, that harmony was quickly disrupted.

Christians have sometimes been inclined to associate sin with the material world, especially the body. They have been tempted to link all "things of the flesh"—for example, the human inclination to be "fleshly minded" rather than "spiritually minded"—with the fall. In this way of thinking, salvation, or redemption from sin, requires Christians to avoid things "of the flesh" in order to "be spiritual."

This, however, is a fundamental misreading of the Genesis story. Nothing in that narrative suggests that physical creation, including the human body, is inherently sinful. There are many ways to describe the nature of sin: as pride, as jealousy, as the human desire for self-sufficiency. But regardless of where you put the emphasis, the consequences of sin are not that it somehow corrupts the material world, but that it divides and isolates. Sin separates creation from the Creator. Sin undoes the essential unity of the spiritual and the material.

In short, sin is best understood as a willful rejection of the incarnation—an undoing of the essential unity between God and creation, and a return to the chaos and void of a world in which God's Spirit and creation are torn asunder.

This becomes clear when we look at the results of sin. Adam and Eve move from a relationship of trust and intimacy into a life that is deeply divided. These divisions take various forms. For example, Adam and Eve are alienated by sin from their own bodies. They begin to look on their bodies as objects, as "things." No longer joined in a trusting relationship with each other or with God, they recognize their nakedness, feel shame, and hide their bodies from each other by putting on clothes.

Even more significantly, Adam and Eve are divided from God. The intimacy that once joined them to the Creator has been called into question, so when God desires to walk with them "in the cool of the day," (Genesis 3:8) Adam and Eve run in the opposite direction.

This same separation of the spiritual from the material also has consequences for how humans relate to the natural world: as a result of sin, humans are inclined to treat nature itself as an object, as something that must be feared, struggled against, exploited, and mastered.

The ultimate expression of this new divide created by sin is Cain's murder of Abel. Blinded by jealousy over Abel's apparent favor with God, Cain begins to look on his brother as an object, a "thing" without any sort of spiritual connection to himself or to God. From a sin-shaped perspective, human beings are merely bodies—time-bound physical objects subject to injury and aging, moving inexorably toward death.

Thankfully, however, this is not the end of the story. Even though the evidence of our separation from each other, from nature, and from God is overwhelming, we also retain a memory of a deeper and truer identity. Somehow, in our bones we know that we were made to live in intimacy with God and with each other. We have been tainted by sin—we are exiles living "east of Eden"—but at the same time we yearn to return home, hoping for a new unity of body and spirit that God intended for us.

The Incarnation: The Hinge of Salvation

How we find our way home to the harmony that God intended at Creation is the central theme of the rest of the Bible. Over and over in the Old Testament, we see God calling a people back to the wholeness of body and spirit for which they were created. God's presence is always made visible in the material, tangible, physical world of creation itself: a burning bush; waters that part at just the right moment; manna that falls miraculously from heaven; a set of commandments physically inscribed in stone; an ark that holds mysterious powers; a temple in which God is said to "dwell."

To be sure, the same Scriptures also repeatedly warn against the temptation of idolatry—the human impulse to worship created things rather than the Creator. Clearly, God cannot be bound by shape or form. Yet God is also never distant or aloof from creation. Repeatedly, the children of Israel call to mind the "mighty acts of God," in which God intervened in history to save them from danger. They prayed fervently for the day when the whole earth would be "filled with the . . . glory of the Lord as the waters cover the sea" (Habakkuk 2:14) or a time to come when "all mankind together will see" the glory of God (Isaiah 40:5). The prophets of Israel yearned for the day when "no one will make them afraid" (Ezekiel 34:28; Zephaniah 3:13). Above all, they looked forward to the full revelation of God in the form of the Anointed One—the Messiah.

When the Messiah did arrive, he did so not as a spiritual abstraction, but in the tangible, physical form of a real human being. The Gospel accounts of Christ's birth are rich in details of time and place. According to Luke, Jesus was born to real parents—Mary and Joseph of Nazareth—in the village of Bethlehem at the time when Quirinius was governor of Syria. Both Luke and Matthew identify Jesus as part of a long genealogical heritage that went all the way back to David. The Gospel stories make it abundantly clear that Jesus was a real, flesh-and-blood human who shared every aspect of ordinary human life. He ate, slept, and drank. He wept when he heard of Lazarus's death. He got mad at the buyers and sellers in the temple. He struggled to control his fear in the garden of Gethsemane. He experienced the anguish of loneliness and rejection. He suffered intense physical pain. And he died a humiliating and painful death.

Yet at the same time, the Gospels also make it clear that Jesus was not "just" another human being. After all, Jesus was born to a virgin. The natural world itself celebrated his birth in the form of a star, and choirs of celestial angels stunned shepherds from the surrounding countryside with hymns of homage and praise to the Christ child. Throughout his ministry, Jesus consistently blurred the line between the physical and the spiritual world. He performed miracles of physical healing. He calmed storms. He cast out demons. He fed whole crowds with a few fish and loaves of bread. And he raised the dead to life again.

In the end, not even death itself could claim the final word. After three days in the grave, Christ arose from the dead, ministered to his disciples for another forty days, and then ascended into heaven.

In Jesus we have the fullest example of what God intended for all of us in creation. The incarnation is the ultimate "do over." Paul's letters go so far as to describe Jesus as the "new Adam." If the story of the first Adam is an account of human brokenness that led to death, the story of Christ as the second Adam is an account of creation being truly restored.

Not surprisingly, the theme of reconciliation and healing was central to Jesus' entire ministry. Wherever he went, in every encounter, Jesus sought to heal what was divided or broken or hurting. The most obvious instances were the miraculous acts of physical healing. But there are also numerous examples of Jesus healing broken minds and spirits, offering new life to those who were spiritually dead, bringing together people who were at odds with each other, restoring dignity to those living in shame or at the margins of respectable society.

Nowhere is this mission of reconciliation expressed more dramatically than in Christ's death and resurrection. The Bible spares us no detail about the reality of his suffering. The pain of the crucifixion was not only physical—the gruesome details of a whipping; nails pounded into his hands and feet; a spear piercing his side—the pain was also emotional. Judas betrayed him; the disciples fell asleep in the garden of Gethsemane; Peter—the Rock on whom the church is supposed to be built—denied him three times. And Christ's suffering went even deeper. Few words in Scripture are more chilling than Jesus' anguished cry on the cross: "My God, My God, why have you forsaken me?" (Matthew 27: 46; Mark 15:34). The Bible makes it unmistakably clear that Jesus suffered in the same way that we suffer and that he died a physical death.

But if the story ended there, it is almost certain that Jesus would be forgotten along with the many other social revolutionaries or wise teachers throughout history. Contrary to the impression given by many Protestant sermons and familiar hymns, the truly powerful part of the story is not the crucifixion, but the resurrection. As it turns out, the physical body of Christ—beaten, crucified, speared, and left for dead—could not be contained in the tomb. The resurrection offers *physical* testimony to the fact that the God who created life is more powerful than the divisive forces of sin and death. In the resurrection, God makes it clear that our bodies are not merely things, that the forces dividing us from each other and from God will not prevail, and that death does not have the final word. In the resurrection, the forces of violence and evil that tore Christ's body apart—forces that seem so powerful in the world today—are defeated.

It is no accident that the Gospels are emphatic that Christ's resurrected body was indeed a physical body. To be sure, the resurrected Jesus walked through walls and could appear or disappear at will. But he was no ghost or ghoul. Almost immediately after the resurrection, he paused to break bread for an evening meal with Cleopas; he allowed Thomas, full of skepticism, to touch his wounded hands and side; he assured the disciples that his body was real; and he ate a breakfast of fried fish with them. Then, forty days after the resurrection, his physical body ascended into heaven, where Christ is now seated at the right hand of the Father.

What's at Stake? Why the Early Church Cared About the Incarnation

Although the early church understood the life, death, and resurrection of Christ in continuity with God's covenant with Israel, the incarnation of Jesus also marked the beginning of a new era of human history. "If anyone is in Christ," wrote the apostle Paul, "there is a new creation: everything old has passed away; see, everything has become new!" (2 Corinthians 5:17 NRSV). The most tangible evidence of this new creation could be seen in the formation of a new community at Pentecost, made possible by the gift of the Holy Spirit and the many "signs and wonders" that accompanied the early church's mission of restoration and healing.

In its life together, this new community became a reminder to the world of God's intention at creation for all of humanity. Here, for example, money was to be shared freely; sins were openly confessed and forgiven; those in authority did not lord over weaker members; barriers between Gentiles and Jews, slaves and free, men and women were broken down; and all people were to be treated with dignity and respect. In this new community, the incarnation found expression in a "new creation" made visible to the world in transformed relationships.

Writers of the New Testament used a rich variety of images to describe how the incarnation of Christ made this reconciliation possible. Some writers, for example, drew on traditional ritual images of *sacrifice*, arguing that the death of an innocent victim served as a substitute for the punishment we deserved. Others appealed to the legal language of *redemption*, with its connotations of being set free or ransomed. Still other writers described Jesus as the giver of *knowledge* (the "true light" of John 1:9), as a *moral example* (see Philippians 2), or as *victorious over the power of evil and death* by disarming "the principalities and powers . . . [and] triumphing over them" (Colossians 2:15).

Recognizing that the gospel message was bigger than the inherited categories of either the Hebrew or Greek culture of his day, Paul introduced his letter to the church at Corinth by openly recognizing that the crucifixion of Christ confounded all the cultural assumptions and scholarly insights of his day. What we are preaching, he insisted, is "a stumbling block to Jews and foolishness to Gentiles" (1 Corinthians 1:23).

Paul regarded the paradox of Christ crucified as a clear strength of the early Christian message. But later Christian theologians felt the need to develop arguments to explain the nature of Jesus in terms that seemed more consistent with the principles of reason. Thus some early Christians, offended by the idea that God could actually become a human being, described Jesus primarily in his divine or spiritual role. This view, sometimes called Docetism (from the Greek *dokei*, "to seem"), argued that Jesus only seemed to be human. Since he existed as God from the beginning of time, the thirty-three years Jesus spent on earth were a momentary disruption to his true spiritual identity. Jesus was a temporary vehicle for the divine Christ-Spirit, but he was never really fully human.

Docetism has found various expressions in the history of the church. One variation especially popular today passes over the three years of Jesus' life on earth—his ministry of healing and teaching—to focus almost exclusively on his divinely appointed role as Savior from our sins. This emphasis on Jesus' divine identity, in turn, tends to regard salvation as primarily an inward, or spiritual, matter of a "changed heart"—inviting Jesus to "come into our hearts." Modern docetism tends to look on Jesus as something of an abstraction, so that the individual, inner experience of having a personal relationship with Jesus is disconnected from a transformed life rooted in daily discipleship.

If docetism is squeamish about the humanity of Christ, a second powerful impulse within early church history moved in the opposite direction by denying that Jesus was fully divine. Arianism—named after Arius, a fourth-century theologian—argues that Jesus was created by God and therefore cannot be thought of as identical with God. After all, if Jesus had a real, physical body, then he could not possibly be divine at the same time. Behind Arius's logic was a deep desire to honor the fundamental character of God. How could God, he argued, who is transcendent, unchanging, eternal, become a human being without being changed in the process?

Contemporary expressions of Arianism tend to describe Jesus as a very good human person, a wise man who may point us to God but who was never anything more than an inspiring teacher. Jesus was extremely gifted and intelligent. His example encourages us to be more godly and his teachings help us better understand God's purposes in the world. In the end, however, Jesus was a lot like us, only much smarter, wiser, and kinder.

The early church struggled with both of these teachings—that Jesus was a God who only seemed to have a body or that Jesus was a nearly perfect human being who appeared to be like God—and ultimately rejected them as heresies. Instead, the church reaffirmed the earliest testimony of the apostles that resolutely linked the crucifixion (Jesus was a real human being who bled, suffered, and died) with the resurrection (Jesus is the Son of God who triumphs over evil and death) and reaffirmed the deep mystery of the incarnation, namely, that Jesus is *fully human* as well as *fully divine.*

In the second century, the church father Irenaeus argued that Jesus "became what we are, so that he might bring us to be even what he is himself,"[1] a teaching often summarized as "he became man so that we might become God." By the fourth century, representatives of the church agreed on a formulation that elevated the paradox of the incarnation to the status of a formal doctrine of the church. Thus, in 325, the Council of Nicea affirmed that Jesus "was of one substance" with God *and* that he "was incarnate and was made man." Several decades later, the Council of Constantinople (381), gave an even more precise formulation, which was refined even further a century later by the Athanasian Creed (ca. 500) to read,

> He is God, begotten before all worlds from the being of the Father, and he is man, born in the world from the being of his mother—existing fully as God, and fully as man with a rational soul and a human body; equal to the Father in divinity, subordinate to the Father in humanity. Although he is God and man, he is not divided, but is one Christ. He is united because God has taken humanity into

himself; he does not transform deity into humanity. He is completely one in the unity of his person, without confusing his natures. For as the rational soul and body are one person, so the one Christ is God and man.

The Incarnation in the Anabaptist-Mennonite Tradition

Anabaptists in the sixteenth century tended to avoid debates about abstract theological concepts. The lived example of Christian discipleship, they taught, was a more effective theological argument than wrangling over the precise wording of church doctrine. When pressed, however, most were quick to insist that their teachings were in full harmony with the doctrines and practices of the early church. And on questions regarding the nature of Christ—particularly the incarnation—the Anabaptists wrote a great deal.

Several early Anabaptist writers, including Menno Simons, confirmed the popular perception of Anabaptists as heretics by defending a variation of Docetism known as the "celestial flesh" of Jesus. But they were exceptions. For most Anabaptists, the early church's understanding of the incarnation was the foundation of their entire theology.

In fact, in contrast to standard Catholic and Protestant approaches, which often began their doctrinal statements with detailed arguments about the nature and character of God, the Anabaptists generally opened their theological reflections with a focus on Jesus. They knew of course, that God is made known to humanity in many ways: through the covenant with Israel or the gift of the Holy Spirit or the words of Scripture. But in the person of Jesus, we find the fullest revelation of God's nature and character.

A summary of Anabaptist convictions on the incarnation would include the following themes.

1. The authority of Jesus for faith and life. The Anabaptist teaching that Jesus was both fully God and fully human underscored their belief in the divine *authority* of Jesus. Whereas some traditions see the character of God as being in tension with the teachings of Christ (especially in contrasting the Old and New Testaments), the Anabaptists insisted that God's will for humanity is revealed most fully in the person of Jesus. Leonhard Schiemer, an early Anabaptist martyr, offered a typical Anabaptist perspective, anchored in a cluster of biblical texts: "In Christ dwells the fullness of the deity. He alone is Lord of all lords and the King of all kings, a Healer and Savior of the human race. To him is given all authority in heaven, on earth and under the earth. Therefore we are properly subject to him, give him our obedience, and honor, fear, and love him above all creatures." Hans Schlaffer, a contemporary of Schiemer and fellow martyr, recognized that accepting Christ as the full revelation of God "is difficult and dangerous to speak about. . . . It scandalizes both Jews and Christians." But Schlaffer cited similar scriptural texts and concluded that "the Word which was with God from the beginning, has become flesh. . . . That is Christ, who says himself: the Father is in me and I am in the Father. I and the Father are one."

The central authority of Christ also shaped the way Anabaptists interpreted Scripture. Wherever a passage in the Bible seemed unclear, Anabaptists insisted that the text should be interpreted through the life and teachings of Jesus. In Christ, for example, the promises of the Old Testament find their fulfillment—the light of Christ's teaching illuminates what had previously been understood only as a shadow, revealing fully God's will for humanity. Thus Christ's command to love our enemies by turning the other cheek or to repay evil with goodness or to "go the second mile" trumped texts in the Old Testament that seemed to contradict these teachings.

This view of the incarnation also underscored the *uniqueness* of Christ. If Jesus is "fully God," there is no other means by which humans can enter into a saving relationship with God. Jesus said, "I am the way and the truth and the life" (John 14:6). Few Christians in the sixteenth century found it necessary to debate this point. But for Mennonites today, the claim is significant. If the incarnation is true, contemporary Christians must reject modern forms of Arianism that reduce Jesus to merely an exemplary model of ethical behavior and be very skeptical of a related tendency to assume all religions are basically pointing toward the same general truth.

2. God is revealed to humans through the material. If the assertions regarding Christ's divine authority seem audacious, the Anabaptist insistence that God is made known to human beings in a material form is equally striking. Some modern Christians have tended to think about their faith in a highly intellectual way, turning Christ into a concept or principle. Others focus on emotions or feelings, thereby making Christ into a spiritual abstraction. These emphases can easily lead to an understanding of Jesus that is fundamentally disconnected from the material world. As a result, Christian faith can be reduced to a set of vague concepts about love, a warm feeling, or a collection of pious-sounding phrases.

For the Anabaptists, the incarnation of Christ was crucial for understanding that God is revealed to humanity. In Jesus, God is made known to the world in material, bodily, visible form.

The implications of this seemingly simple claim are profound. For skeptics, it means that the account of Jesus' life, death, and resurrection is not simply a great parable; it is a true story anchored in concrete details of the created world. God literally entered into human history. To spiritualists, it means that created things are *essential* to God's self-revelation. Indeed, without this physical, flesh-and-blood, human Jesus—a Christ crowned with thorns and hanging on the cross—God could not be fully known to humanity, and we could not find salvation. In other words, God's Spirit is never just an abstraction or a feeling. God is revealed through the medium of material forms. Like radio waves, the Word of the Lord is silent until it is translated into the physical world. This need not diminish the power or the authority of the message; it does not reduce the message to medium. But it does firmly anchor our talk about God, the Holy Spirit, and the presence of Christ within the material world.

This perspective has significant implications for how we think about the created world in general. God has pronounced creation good! It is the means by which God becomes visible in the world. Since the incarnation of Christ demonstrates that God uses material forms to become visible to the world, then everything in the world, including our bodies, is precious—a potential means through which God could enter history.

3. The meaning of salvation: participation in Christ through the Holy Spirit. This understanding of the incarnation of God in Christ also had profound implications for the Anabaptists' view of salvation, particularly the possibility of a genuine transformation of life (what some later Christians were to call "sanctification"). The Anabaptists certainly did not ignore the fall. Indeed, they were very clear about the pervasiveness of human sin. But the biblical story, they taught, begins in Genesis 1, not in Genesis 3. Yes, the power of Satan is real, and the natural order has been profoundly injured by sin. But we were designed by a loving and gracious God to live in harmony with God, with each other, and with creation. And because the Word was made flesh in Christ, redemption is possible not only in an abstract, spiritual sense, but in a more concrete way as well.

A favorite Anabaptist text describes this relationship with the image of a flourishing plant. Jesus says to his followers, "I am the vine, you are the branches. He who abides in Me, and I in him, bears much fruit; for without Me you can do nothing. . . . By this My Father is glorified, that you bear much fruit; so you will be My disciples" (John 15:5, 8 NKJV). Through the Holy Spirit, Christians can participate in the body of Christ. In so doing, our own bodies, thoughts, and actions can also be redeemed.

Sometimes the Anabaptists were falsely accused of ignoring the role of grace in salvation, of turning faith into "works righteousness." To the contrary, Anabaptists almost always described salvation as a gift offered by God freely and without conditions. But they also insisted that Christian faith was not merely a passive or legal matter of being "justified" before God. Rather, in Christ, we are invited to participate in the life-giving Spirit of God. When, through the presence of the Holy Spirit, Christians are made alive in Christ—as branches of the vine—they are also "made righteous" and are expected to bear the fruit of that righteousness. In other words, grace not only justifies us before God, but also sanctifies and empowers us to accomplish the will of God. The world is full of Christians, the Anabaptist Pilgram Marpeck wrote, "who confess only the mortal and physical Christ, but very few believe and confess the risen Christ with their lives."

In the Anabaptist-Mennonite understanding, this is salvation: to participate fully in the incarnation of Christ, both in his *humanity* and, through the presence of the Spirit, in his *divinity*. As the apostle Paul put it, "We know that our old self was crucified with him so that the body of sin might be done away with, that we should no longer be enslaved to sin. . . . For sin shall not be your master, because you are not under law, but under grace" (Romans 6:6, 14).

4. The church as the body of Christ visible today. Finally, the doctrine of the incarnation was also central to the Anabaptist understanding of the church. Jesus promised his followers that "where two or three come together in my name, there I am with them" (Matthew 18:20). The apostles and the early church went even further to speak of the church as the body of Christ. Christ is no longer physically present on earth, of course, but he lives on in the tangible, visible form of the gathered community of faith that bears his name. Thus the primary expression of God's presence in the world today is the church, where the Spirit is "embodied" by disciples of Christ who heed his teachings, who participate in the fellowship of his suffering, and who bear witness in their lives to the hope of his resurrection. Pilgram Marpeck once described the church as the "prolongation of the incarnation." By this, he meant that the incarnation is not an "event" that happened once upon a time. Rather, the resurrected Jesus remains alive in the world today in the regenerated lives of faithful believers.

Clearly, the presence of the Holy Spirit was essential to the church if it was to be the body of Christ. The church depended on the inward active movement of the Spirit, transforming the hearts and minds of believers. This meant that the church could not be reduced to a list of programs, a set of prescribed behaviors, or carefully formulated doctrines.

At the same time, the Anabaptists rejected the arguments of the spiritualists of their day who described Jesus in abstract language as "glorified" and "transfigured," departed to a distant heaven. No, they claimed. The body of Christ has a visible form still today. As in the time of Jesus, we are still called to follow; to relax our grip on our resources of time, money, and talents; and to put loyalty to Christ above all other allegiances, including the state, the market, and even our families.

Conclusion

In all of these ways, the Anabaptist-Mennonite tradition incorporated the central teachings of the Christian church into the core of its theology. Because Christ is the Word made flesh, he is the authoritative standard for Christian life and biblical interpretation. Because Christ is the Word made flesh, we have confidence that the created world can be redeemed. Because Christ is the Word made flesh, we can participate in him and bear the fruit of a sanctified and holy life. And because Christ is the Word made flesh, we can gather for worship as the body of Christ and bear witness in our lives that the incarnation of God in Christ continues to be good news to the world.

The world in which we live is filled with broken, divided, lonely, and alienated people—a condition that is only made worse by the deep currents of modern culture. The good news of the gospel is that Jesus has come to break down the dividing walls of hostility. In Jesus, God became one with humanity. The mission of the church is to testify to the incarnation by inviting all those who are broken, divided, lonely, and alienated into the joy of new life, nourished by the vine of Christ, and bearing the fruit of reconciliation and wholeness.

3

Remembering Who(se) We Are

Why Worship Matters

One of the many pleasures of teaching at a small, church-related college is the opportunity to develop relationships with students beyond the classroom. Recently, I had a several conversations with a young man who was thinking about life after graduation. Initially, we focused on the standard topics of career and work opportunities. The student was bright and talented, with many options. But soon the conversation turned to the deeper questions of meaning and purpose.

Like many students I encounter, he had been raised in a Mennonite church and baptized as a teenager. While in high school, he participated in several short-term service assignments and in two denominational youth conventions, which he described as spiritual high points. At college he took numerous Bible and religion courses, enthusiastically joined in campus hymn sings, and clearly considered himself to be a Christian.

But when I asked him where he was attending church, he stammered a bit and then confessed that he had not been going anywhere. After a few exploratory visits during his freshman year, Sunday worship simply had no appeal to him. When I pressed the question further, he finally blurted out, "I just don't see the point. After I came to college, I realized that I had been going to church just out of habit, because my parents made me. But when I quit attending, I found that I didn't really miss it all that much." Then he added, "Besides, I feel closer to God taking a walk along the millrace than I ever did in church on Sunday morning."

My initial response was one of bewilderment, tinged with exasperation. Why would a person who has been so deeply grounded in the church all his life, who has made a public commitment of baptism, and who wants to think about his future as a "calling," regard congregational life as irrelevant? How can you be a Christian and not gather on a regular basis with like-minded people for worship?

Yet even as I professed my surprise, I knew that my friend was not alone. According to recent surveys, church attendance by young adults has been steadily declining in nearly every denomination for the past thirty years. Whereas the mean age of Mennonites in 1989 was forty-nine, by 2006 it had climbed to fifty-four. In 1972, 54 percent of Mennonites were between the ages of eighteen and forty-five; in 1989 this number had declined to 45 percent; by 2006 it had fallen to 30 percent. Mainline Protestant churches, one prominent researcher has argued, are "literally dying out."

In his book *They Like Jesus But Not the Church*, Dan Kimball summarizes the perceptions of a growing number of young adults toward the church. Most have a generally positive attitude toward Jesus, his study suggests. They are, on the whole, keenly interested in religion and are eager to explore issues related to spirituality. Yet their attitudes toward the church itself tend to be quite negative. The church is judgmental and arrogant. It pursues a narrow political agenda that is, among other things, homophobic and oppressive to women. The church is filled with fundamentalists who insist that every word in the Bible must be taken literally.

Naturally, most readers who hear these charges are likely to react as I did: "This is ridiculous! These caricatures are just wrong! This doesn't describe my congregation!" And yet, whether we agree with the perceptions or not, fundamental shifts are taking place across the Christian church. Whereas regular church attendance a generation ago could simply be taken for granted in many communities, today that assumption no longer holds, especially among young people. And if our only response is a defensive insistence that our congregation is somehow different, we are not likely to respond effectively to the profound transformations that are happening in our midst.

In the previous chapter, I argued that the Christian doctrine of the incarnation is foundational to an Anabaptist-Mennonite understanding of salvation. In this chapter, I want to explore how we move from an intellectual understanding of the incarnation to a deeper encounter with the mystery of the Word made flesh, focusing especially on worship. Why *does* worship matter? Why is it necessary to gather on a regular basis with other Christians to sing, pray, read, and reflect? And, though it gets ahead of the story a bit, just how is worship relevant to our daily lives or the deep currents of our culture?

The reflections that follow are only a beginning response to those questions, but I hope they suggest some useful directions for further conversation.

Anabaptist-Mennonite Ambivalence About Worship

Convincing young people of the importance of attending church on Sunday morning is a challenge in every denomination. But it is made somewhat more difficult for contemporary Mennonites by a deep historical suspicion in the Anabaptist tradition regarding ritual forms of worship. If you ask random Catholics to describe something distinctive about their faith, their answer would almost certainly include some reference to mass. Ask Lutherans, and they will probably say something about "word and sacrament." Ask a Pentecostal, and you will likely hear some reference to speaking in tongues.

But ask Mennonites to describe something distinctive about their faith, and it is highly improbable that the answer will have anything to do with worship practices. You might hear a passing reference to a rich tradition of four-part singing, but Mennonites are much more likely to talk about the peace witness, a commitment to service, or a strong sense of community as distinctive markers of their denominational tradition than about any activity associated with Sunday morning worship.

The reasons behind this ambivalence are deeply rooted in history. Sixteenth-century Anabaptism emerged, in part at least, as a reaction against medieval Catholic worship practices that seemed mechanical and idolatrous. The first generation of Anabaptists denounced the elaborate pageantry and images associated with the Catholic mass. The enormous cathedrals with their elaborately carved altars, the gold chalices, stained-glass windows, baptismal fonts, statues of the saints, shrines to Virgin Mary, and relics—all this seemed both wasteful and theologically misguided. The Catholic focus on relics, holy places, and the lives of the saints, so the Anabaptists claimed, encouraged a kind of idol worship. The towering cathedrals with their ornate decorations were built on the backs of an impoverished peasantry kept firmly under the control of the clergy. Above all, the Anabaptists believed that the Catholic Church's defining rituals—infant baptism and the mass—were not supported by Scripture. To become an Anabaptist in the sixteenth century, therefore, meant an explicit rejection of these outward images and ritual forms of worship.

At the heart of the Anabaptist critique of Catholic worship practices was a fundamental disagreement about the nature of the sacraments. In Catholic practice, ordinary people came into the presence of God—they experienced salvation—through the sacraments of the church. The sacrament of baptism, for example, washed away the taint of original sin and ultimately assured the infant of eternal life in heaven. In the sacrament of communion, Catholics came into the actual presence of Christ, who was made physically present in the elements of the bread and wine. Since a sacrament was valid only when administered by an ordained priest, the institutional hierarchy of the church seemingly held a kind of monopoly over salvation.

The Anabaptists rejected these sacramental teachings. God, they argued, is present in all of creation, not just in the water of baptism or the bread and wine of communion. Because all time is holy and all space is sanctified, the kind of worship God most desires is not to be found in ceremonies or rituals or beautiful cathedrals, but in a life lived in obedience to Christ. The Anabaptists were familiar with the words of the prophet Micah:

With what shall I come before the LORD and bow down before the exalted God? Shall I come before him with burnt offerings, with calves a year old? Will the LORD be pleased with thousands of rams, with ten thousand rivers of oil? Shall I offer my firstborn for my transgression, the fruit of my body for the sin of my soul? He has showed you, O man, what is good. And what does the LORD require of you? To act justly and to love mercy and to walk humbly with your God. (Micah 6:6-8)

These reservations about Catholic forms of worship were only reinforced by the fact that Anabaptists were often compelled to meet in secret, hidden from church and civil authorities who were ready to kill them for their teachings. Thus early Anabaptist worship services were often furtive gatherings held in back rooms, barns, caves, or forest clearings, usually at odd hours of the day, in the knowledge that their worship could be disrupted at any time by an angry neighbor or the local sheriff.

As a result of this enforced secrecy, we know very little about the details of early Anabaptist worship. In 1527, the Swiss Brethren circulated a simple "Congregational Order" that outlined the basic structure of their worship practices. "The brothers and sisters should meet at least three or four times a week," the order exhorted, for the purpose of reading and interpreting Scriptures together, encouraging each other in the faith, and admonishing each other if a member had fallen astray. The order also suggested that members would share their possessions generously with each other. And it called for the regular observance of the Lord's Supper to remember Christ's suffering and as a reminder "that we might also be called to give our body and life . . . for the sake of all the brothers."

In an eyewitness account of an Anabaptist worship service from 1557, Elias Schad, a Lutheran vicar from Strasbourg, reported that some two hundred Anabaptists from near and far had met secretly at night in a forest clearing just outside the city.[2] After a series of short sermons from the Epistles, the participants knelt and began to pray, "murmuring as if a nest of hornets were swarming." During the sermons "some were standing, some were leaning against trees, many were seated, many lay on their sides, some lay face down, some were napping and some even sleeping." Then, after a lengthy period of prayer, the elders extended general greetings to the participants and invited the group to raise questions related to the sermon. If the Spirit so led, those present could also offer "something to edify the brethren." The meeting finally broke up at two a.m. Schad's report conforms reasonably well to several other accounts of secret Anabaptist worship services, although two descriptions from the region of Hesse in 1578 included singing, baptism, and the practice of the Lord's Supper.[3]

Even though Mennonites continued to be skeptical about formal liturgical rituals, over time their worship practices assumed a recognizable structure and pattern. Today, a typical Mennonite worship service would likely include a welcome, several hymns, an offering, a Scripture reading, the sermon, a period of open congregational sharing, general announcements, and a sending benediction, interspersed with several occasions for prayer. But apart from this basic form, contemporary Mennonite worship practices are governed more by the weight of local custom than by a highly conscious theological rationale. On any given Sunday, people in the same Mennonite congregation likely gather with varying expectations about what they are hoping to encounter: an emotional experience of joy, an intellectual challenge to ponder, a deep encounter with Scripture, practical counsel regarding relationships, or admonitions on ethical behavior.

In general, most Mennonites would not be inclined to think of worship as the primary focus of the Christian faith. At their best, Mennonites have assumed that the form of worship most pleasing to God is a life conformed to the teachings of Jesus and a church whose members model this way of life to the world around. Mennonite worship, then, tends to celebrate God's presence in the gathering of the community and in a life of daily discipleship. At its worst, however, Mennonite worship has come to mean "going to church"—a dry, routine habit driven primarily by the force of tradition or the discomfort of guilt. When this is the case, young people legitimately ask "why bother," especially when they can find community in the local volleyball league, service opportunities in any number of local community organizations, and spiritual inspiration from the music list on their IPod.

Hunger for Worship and Renewal

This description may seem far too pessimistic, in part because so many congregations have recently taken steps to reinvigorate worship with new energy. Nowhere has this been more evident than in the area of music. In many Mennonite churches today, the worship hour begins with an extended period of singing. Often a praise team of five or six people—usually equipped with microphones, guitars, a piano, and a drum set—leads the congregation in a series of upbeat songs borrowed from the growing contemporary Christian music scene. The lyrics of these songs are projected onto a screen for all to see, thereby lifting eyes out of the hymnals and freeing hands for clapping or similar expressions of praise.

Other Mennonite congregations have tried to invigorate the worship hour by moving more in the direction of "high church" worship practices. These congregations tend to structure their worship themes around the common lectionary readings and the liturgical seasons of the church year. They often incorporate art and dance into the worship space and may supplement their hymns with music from the Taizé or the Iona communities.

None of these initiatives have come without internal conflict and resistance. But the intensity of debate in many Mennonite congregations today over what happens on Sunday morning is an indication that something important is at stake.

Contemporary Mennonites have a profound hunger for meaningful worship, a deep desire to encounter the holy. In the absence of much explicit guidance from the Anabaptist tradition, however, efforts to renew worship have tended to result in a willy-nilly borrowing from across the Christian spectrum—mingling the good, the bad, and sometimes even the ugly—in the hopes of eventually hitting on the right formula.

Why Does Worship Matter?

Finding our way through the current confusion may be helped if we first take a step back to reflect on some more basic questions. What, for example, do we have to say to the young man in my office who asks, why *does* worship matter? Why should we expect the habits of worship inherited from the past to connect with people today? Why not, as he suggested, consider a walk in the park as a sufficient form of worship?

In recent years, a wide range of Christians, including some Mennonites, have given a great deal of thought to these questions. Not everyone agrees, of course, on what aspect of worship deserves the most attention. Here I will simply highlight four specific themes that seem to be recurring in these conversations, saving a fifth theme as the primary focus of the following chapter.

1. God is worthy of praise. Though it may not immediately convince my skeptical student, the most powerful reason for worship is also the simplest: Christians gather for worship because it is the appropriate response to the One who has created us, given us the gift of life, and invited us to participate in the healing of creation.

In some ways, all other explanations for worship are superfluous. Worship is nothing more than the appropriate response to a God who loves us and desires to be in relationship with us. It is as natural and necessary to human well-being as breathing oxygen or eating nutritious food. Thus, at its most fundamental level, worship is not about us or our churches, our rituals, our traditions, or even our feelings. It is simply a conscious response of gratitude and praise for God's goodness, grace, and glory.

This posture of praise should permeate everything we do, in every waking moment of our day. Indeed, the Psalms are filled with spontaneous expressions of praise that seem to be triggered by nothing more than an awareness of the inherent goodness of God: "Come, let us bow down in worship, let us kneel before the Lord our Maker" (Psalm 95:6); "Taste and see that the Lord is good" (Psalm 34:8); "My lips will shout for joy when I sing praises to you—I, whom you have redeemed" (Psalm 71:23). In the words of the Book of Common Prayer, "it is . . . our bounden duty, that we should at all time, and in all places, give thanks."

Because human beings are so forgetful—so easily distracted by our own priorities and the concerns of the moment—it is also appropriate to set aside special times and particular places for praising God. In formal worship, Christians are especially attentive to the content of their spoken words, to the claims made in their hymns, to the gestures made to each other, and to the physical space and visual images that surround and enhance our praise. These rituals are not ends in themselves but simply helpful ways to focus attention and to offer a collective expression of thanksgiving. Rituals of worship provide regular reminders of our proper relationship to God. Through the rhythms of worship, our praise spills out beyond the formal worship hour to permeate every part of our lives.

2. Worship names our ultimate allegiances. A slightly different way of saying this is that worship names our most basic assumptions about reality and, therefore, our ultimate allegiances. As we gather to sing, read Scripture, confess, pray, preach, and share, we collectively express our most fundamental convictions about life's meaning and purpose. At its heart, worship is a public proclamation about sovereignty and allegiance. In this sense, it is a *political* act.

If it sounds strange to think of worship in the language of politics, it may be because modern westerners, in the United States especially, are so used to making a sharp division between the *sacred* (the spiritual world of piety, worship, and prayer) and the *secular* (the everyday world of work, politics, and economics). What people do on Sunday morning, we tend to assume, is about sacred matters. Because it focuses on religious concerns, worship is personal and private—a matter of the heart. But once we move into the workplace during the rest of the week, a different set of assumptions apply that have nothing to do with worship.

This distinction between the sacred and the secular—between what happens on Sunday morning and the "realities" of life during the other six days of the week—is pervasive in modern culture, often in ways we scarcely recognize. What we often overlook, however, is the fact that all of us are *always* engaged in worship of one sort or another. That is, all of us—even the most secular people—are deeply committed to a particular understanding of reality that guides our assumptions, attitudes, and actions. Consider, for example, those people who gather regularly for worship on Sunday afternoon in sports cathedrals where, together with eighty thousand fellow congregants, they enter into a shared ritual experience, sometimes including singing and dancing, and are transported into ecstasies of joy or brought face-to-face with the painful reality of human limitations. For other people, shopping is a kind of worship experience, a ritual practice of entering into a mall—shaped by the catechism of advertisements and the hymns of marketing jingles that come unbidden into our minds—in anticipation of finding comfort, companionship, or the brief ecstasy of a purchase. Or consider the complex relation that citizens have to the nation, in which the ritual pageantry of a Fourth of July parade or the Pledge of Allegiance recited daily by millions of schoolchildren or the national anthem sung reverently, like a hymn, before sporting events can become "liturgical practices" in a form of worship that binds us to the nation and its story about human nature and destiny.

Precisely because worship is about sovereignty and expressions of allegiance, the Bible is full of warnings against idolatry: it is possible to worship false gods! If these concerns are real—if Christians can be led astray by the appeal of false gods—we should think of worship as an occasion to resist these seductions. In worship we proclaim our loyalty to the One True God and allow ourselves to be formed anew in our identity as members of the body of Christ.

Because we are forgetful people, worship serves as a regular opportunity to name publicly our deepest allegiances.

3. Worship helps us to see the world truthfully. To say it in still another way: we gather for worship to learn how to tell the truth. All of us carry in our minds—often at a barely conscious level—a set of assumptions that help bring structure and coherence to a world that otherwise presents itself to us as chaotic and confusing. The stories that help to order our world are often handed down to us as children from parents and the formative cultural settings of our youth. But these stories are never permanently fixed. Indeed, every day we are surrounded by many different voices—those of friends, co-workers, politicians, advertisements, talk shows, magazines, movies, and so on—all competing to be our guides through the complexities of life. These voices tell us a story about how the world works. They offer a narrative that simplifies life in ways that seem to "make sense."

The problem, however, is that many of these voices turn out to be false friends: the promise that dressing in the latest fashion will make people like you, for example, or that alcohol will make it easier to be intimate, or that dieting will make you a better person. Perhaps no voice is more persuasive in our world right now than the argument that evil can be addressed only with force, and behind that, an even deeper assumption that violence is ultimately the motor that drives human history. To be sure, we rarely make this argument explicitly, and most people hope that violence—even in a righteous cause—will be kept to a minimum. Yet even though we might despise terrorists for using violence or torture, many Christians are ready to defend their own use of violence in the "war on terror," since it is so clearly intended for a good end. The fact that violence is seen as a "tool of last resort"—as the trump card to be played when everything else has failed—is a measure of how deeply rooted this voice is in our minds. And if our primary sources about the nature of reality come from Hollywood movies or political speeches or radio talk shows, we can easily begin to assume that this view of the world is actually true—that the outcome of world history really does finally hinge on our "good use" of violence.

Christian worship challenges this, and many other stories about reality, by offering us an account of creation, life, and human destiny that is simply truer and more honest than all of these other accounts. The biblical story is true in that it accurately describes not only our deepest desire for communion with God, but also our persistent inclination toward selfishness, violence, and sin. We are, all of us, refugees from Eden. The fog and illusions of sin have alienated us from each other and from God.

Yet we also carry with us a memory of the true purpose for

which God created us. In Christ, we are offered a path toward the wholeness and healing that we desire. In his life of love and vulnerability—even in the face of ugly violence and a death on the cross—Christ exposed the logic of coercion as empty foolishness, as the "wisdom of the world." In his resurrection, Christ emerged victorious over the power of fear and violence, and he invites us to participate with him in the healing of our confused and broken world. Christian worship tells a story about reality in which the resurrection triumphs over death, and that story empowers us to live as if God's kingdom is already here, even as we wait with patience and hope for the culmination of history in Christ's return.

We gather on Sunday morning to tell that story because it is a true story. The story we rehearse in worship exposes our illusion that we—rather than God—are in control of human history, and it reminds us how to live in a world infused with God's presence.

What might this look like in actual practice? On the Sunday morning following September 11, 2001, my small congregation in Indiana gathered, as did millions of other Christians around the world, for a service of worship, reflection, and remembrance. At a time when pundits of every sort were debating the appropriate military response to the catastrophe, we asked God for help in understanding the events of the world from a divine perspective. How, in the grand sweep of God's actions in history, should we respond to our new sense of fear and vulnerability? What might Christ have to teach us about the painful reality of violence and suffering in our world?

During the course of our service, we shared many songs, thoughts, prayers, and admonitions. But the memory that has lingered with me the longest, looping repeatedly through my mind in the weeks that followed, was a fragment of a song whose text comes from the Iona community in Scotland:

> Don't be afraid. My love is stronger.
> My love is stronger than your fear.
> Don't be afraid. My love is stronger,
> And I have promised, promised to be always near.

To be sure, there is nothing particularly new or profound in those words. After all, trust in God is the very foundation of Christian faith. The Scriptures are full of admonitions to put our faith in Christ, to rely on God alone, to cast aside our fears in the knowledge of God's presence and strength. Yet by publicly proclaiming in our worship that God's love is stronger than our fear, my congregation was naming a conviction about the direction of human history that is more true, more trustworthy, than the culture's default impulse of calling for patriotic unity and a steely determination to exact "an eye for an eye."

Human beings are by nature extremely forgetful creatures. Left to our own devices, we are easily distracted, flitting like hummingbirds from one thing to the next, lured by appeals that speak directly to our immediate physical and emotional needs. Yet these appeals often turn out to be illusions—lies that only lead us to further confusion, paralysis, and despair.

Sunday morning worship helps us to see the world truthfully, to recall *who* we are and to remember *whose* we are.

4. Worship as the gathering of a new community: the body of Christ. Thus far, I have suggested that worship is about offering praise to God, declaring our deepest allegiances, and discovering what it means to live truthfully in the world. But why would we have to go to church to do these things? Why not simply do all this in the privacy of our own homes or in a leisurely walk in the woods? The answer to that question suggests another crucial dimension of worship. In worship, the gathered body of believers is transformed by the Spirit into the body of Christ. In gathering for worship, we encounter the risen Christ.

When most of us hear the word *church*, the first image that comes to mind is probably a building or maybe the Sunday morning worship service. "Going to church" means showing up at a house of worship where we sit in a pew for ninety minutes as the worship service unfolds. The New Testament word for *church*, however, suggests something much more vivid, dynamic, and participatory. *Ekklesia* in the New Testament means a people who are "called out" for a special task or purpose.

Throughout Scripture, God's fundamental gift of redemption—God's plan to restore creation to its intended wholeness—focuses on calling out a people and inviting them to live together in the way God intended. Thus, in Genesis 12 we read of God's call to Abraham to leave the comfort and prosperity of his home for a distant country that God would show him. The deal was clear: if Abraham would put his trust in God alone, if he was willing to live as God instructed, then God would bless him with many descendents and make his offspring a blessing to the whole world.

The rest of the Old Testament is an ongoing account of God patiently and persistently restoring creation—offering salvation—by calling Abraham and Sarah's descendants to model for the world a life together that reflects the goodness, mercy, and love of God. This was to be a community unified around a public law—the Ten Commandments—given by God as a gift, to be followed by everyone regardless of status. In this community, the political power of kings must be tempered by the qualities of justice and righteousness. In this community, people were to regard the land as a gift from God, to be held as a long-term lease rather than a private possession. Indeed, every fifty years, the community was to proclaim a year of jubilee, when economic and social equality was restored. As a called-out people, the children of Israel were to reflect the character of the God they worshipped in their hospitality to strangers and foreigners, their compassion for widows and orphans, and their generosity to the poor.

Christ came into the world in the context of this called-out people. From the very beginning of his ministry, Jesus assured his listeners that he did not intend to destroy the law of Israel, but rather to help the community fulfill the law in its deepest intention. It was not enough, Jesus insisted, to merely follow the letter of the law—loving those who love you, paying back debts on schedule, or avoiding adultery. After all "even 'sinners' love those who love them" (Luke 6:32). Nor was it simply a matter of becoming "more spiritual" or pious; the Sermon on the Mount did not culminate in a call to focus on one's "personal relationship with God."

Instead, Christ challenged the people of God to be truly called out from the world by living in relationships of love, trust, and generosity. Salvation was made visible to the world in the life of a transformed community. The markers of this transformed community included such practices as giving to all who asked, turning the other cheek, putting trust in God rather than in treasures on earth, being a servant, visiting prisoners, caring for the sick, and offering a cup of cold water. The practices of this new community were so unusual that others took note. Indeed, Jewish leaders and Roman authorities found them so unsettling that they agreed Jesus had to be put to death.

God was still not finished, however. Before the resurrected Christ ascended into heaven, he assured his disciples that he would continue to be present with them. The book of Acts tells the remarkable story of how God's gift of salvation was once again made visible in the form of a called-out people. Infused by the power of the Holy Spirit at Pentecost, the disciples who gathered in Jerusalem were transformed into a new community. Almost immediately the disciples began to bridge cultural divides with the divine gift of new languages.

Members of the early church shared their possessions freely as others had need (see Acts 2, 4). Early on, the group created the special office of deacon, whose task it was to make sure that the needs of the widows and the poor were being addressed. This was a community where people found healing—emotional, spiritual, and physical healing. Like Jesus, the apostles raised people from the dead, cast out demons, restored people to their right minds, and helped to restore broken relationships. Wherever they went, they sought to bring together that which was broken or divided or hurting.

Perhaps the biggest challenge to the early church was the deep division between Jewish followers of Christ and the Greek-speaking converts regarding Jewish cultural traditions and ritual practices. The Jewish followers of Jesus assumed that they had joined a renewal movement within Judaism, based on God's original covenant with Abraham and deeply anchored in Jewish culture, language, and tradition. If converts wanted to join, they could, but only if they were ready to adopt the ritual practices of the Jewish tradition. Gentile converts, on the other hand, understood themselves to be part of a new thing, a called-out community guided exclusively by the teachings of Christ and the presence of the Holy Spirit.

The fate of the church's future hung in the balance as leaders gathered at the so-called Jerusalem Council to address the question head-on. Could God's covenant to a called-out people survive translation into other cultures and other languages? The issue was not easily resolved. But the basic direction was unequivocally clear: in Christ "there is no Greek or Jew, circumcised or uncircumcised, barbarian, Scythian, slave or free" (Colossians 3:11). In Christ the walls of hostility that divided human beings from each other were broken down. In Christ, strangers and foreigners, rich and poor, educated and uneducated joined together as brothers and sisters. Here all people could expect to be treated with respect and dignity, and each person had distinctive gifts to contribute to the body of Christ.

The blessing given to Abraham's descendents was meant to be shared with all peoples—it was a blessing "for the nations," not a treasure to be hoarded. The gift of community was intended for the redemption of the whole world. "The promise is for you and your children and for all who are far off—for all whom the Lord our God will call" (Acts 2:39). Through the presence of the Spirit, the resurrected Christ continued to be present in the church (*ekklesia*), recognized as the body of Christ. In the quality of their life together—sharing possessions, healing of body and mind, reconciling people across cultural divides—the church was missional, testifying to the world that it had been transformed by the Spirit into the living body of Christ and inviting those who are still trapped in patterns of sin and violence to leave behind their old ways, to become disciples of Jesus and members of this new community.

Worship, then, marks the identity of a people who have been called out by God, a people whose life together makes the presence of Christ visible in the world.

A matter of fundamental importance is at stake here. As Jesus made clear, no one "can serve two masters" (see Matthew 6:24; Luke

16:13). Worship clarifies the sharp divide between the unredeemed world and the called-out church, between the kingdom of darkness and the kingdom of light, between Christ and Belial. Therefore, worship is not for the half-hearted, the disinterested, the bored, the guilt-driven, or the creatures of habit.

The invitation to identify with this community is genuine; it can be accepted or denied. No one is "born" into the church in the Anabaptist-Mennonite tradition; no one is coerced into worship. But those who gather for worship do so as a community made visible to the world by its distinctive practices. In this sense, the church, by definition, is always engaged in missions.

Conclusion: Worship as Gathered Form of Witness

The majestic cathedrals that dominate the landscape of virtually every major European city are nearly empty today. People there have not ceased to worship, but in a culture with so many competing claims on time, energy, and resources, they have simply chosen to worship other things. When Christians gather to worship, they are declaring their allegiance to the God of Abraham and Sarah, who is revealed most fully in Jesus Christ. In retelling this story, Christians see their world more clearly, more truthfully.

Worship in the Anabaptist-Mennonite tradition is an inherently corporate act in which the church, in its life together, embodies the wholeness and unity that God intended for all humanity. Worship identifies people who have been called out to live in relationships of love, trust, vulnerability, and intimacy, living now as a foretaste of the restoration of all creation at the great wedding banquet of the Lamb. Gathering for worship is therefore the basis for Christian witness in the world. Practices of worship are literally practice for being in the world; they point to the fact that all of life is worship.

4

Participating in the Incarnation

Christian Worship Practices and Witness

> "Your kingdom come, your will be done on earth as it is in heaven."
>
> —MATTHEW 6:10

> We are what we repeatedly do. Excellence, then, is not an act, but a habit.
>
> —ARISTOTLE

> The key to mission is always worship. . . . You can only be reflecting the love of God into the world if you are worshipping the true God who creates the world out of the overflowing of self-giving love. . . . The more you look at that God and celebrate that love, the more you have to be reflecting that overflowing self-giving love into the world.
>
> —N. T. WRIGHT[4]

On the morning of October 2, 2006, a thirty-three-year-old milk truck driver from Lancaster County, Pennsylvania, affectionately hugged his two oldest children as they boarded a school bus. He then made a brief stop at a local hardware before driving his pickup truck to the front door of a one-room, Amish schoolhouse near the hamlet of Nickel Mines. What happened next still seems to defy imagination. After ordering most of the building's inhabitants to leave, the man tied ten Amish schoolgirls together on the floor. Then, as police gathered outside the school, Charles Carl Roberts IV did the unthinkable: he systematically shot ten little children—ultimately killing five of them—before taking his own life.

Despite its exotic setting, the story of the Amish shootings at the West Nickel Mines schoolhouse seemed initially to follow a painfully familiar storyline. Since the Columbine massacre in 1999, there have been dozens of additional school shootings in the United States, including the thirty-three killed in 2007 at Virginia Tech. Moreover, images of cruel and violent deaths—either on the evening news or in the numbing variety of TV shows that pass for entertainment—have become standard fare in American media.

What stunned the watching world in the days following the shooting was less the reality of horrific violence than the response of the Amish community. Within hours of the tragedy, various Amish spokespersons, including members of the families directly affected by the massacre, were speaking the language of forgiveness. That same evening, a steady stream of Amish visitors came to the home of Amy Roberts, the widow of the gunman, to offer condolences. "Stay in your home here," an Amish delegation told her shortly thereafter. "We have forgiven your husband . . . and we share in your sorrow." "We shouldn't think evil of the man who did this," a grandfather of one of the victims admonished his children standing at the girl's grave. "He too is a child of God."

Although some commentators raised questions about the appropriateness of the forgiveness extended by the Amish community, most people reacted with admiration. Within a week, more than two thousand news stories had been published worldwide on the theme of forgiveness. Many expressed amazement that half of the seventy people who attended the burial of Charles Carl Roberts IV were Amish. Others noted with bewilderment that the committee overseeing public donations had announced that a portion of the money would be set aside in a trust fund for the Roberts family.

Making the story even more confounding was the Amish refusal to frame the response as "heroic." Over and over, they insisted that their reaction to these murders was not extraordinary; they were simply responding as they had done in many other less-publicized instances of criminal wrongdoing against them. Indeed, one could cite dozens of cases in which Amish families and communities extended forgiveness to those responsible for the injury or death of loved ones, often reaching out to develop ongoing relationships with the families of perpetrators. In almost no instances have the Amish accepted financial payments in wrongful death cases.

If people have heard about the Amish at all, they are likely to regard them as an intriguing but ultimately irrelevant sideshow in the rich drama of American culture—fascinating to observe but hardly a model worth imitating. Yet the global outpouring of affirmation for the Amish gesture of forgiveness made it clear that in a world resigned to endless cycles of violence, the possibility of unmerited forgiveness may be relevant after all.

In that gesture of forgiveness, the world came face-to-face with the good news of the gospel. This was a powerful form of witness, clearly rooted in Christian faith, but a witness demonstrated rather than argued. To a culture deeply suspicious of the claims of Christianity, the simple clarity and specificity of the Amish response testified to the redemptive power of love, even in the face of violent death.

This chapter proposes that what Christians have traditionally called *ethics* is really nothing more than the practices of worship expressed as salt and light to the world. In a similar way, what Christians have traditionally called *mission* is simply worship made visible in the world. All three of these themes—worship, ethics, and witness—are united, I suggest here, by the concept of *practices*. Christian witness to the world begins not with a series of persuasive arguments or a strategy for mission but with practices of worship that become embodied in the practices of our daily lives.

How Do We Become Virtuous?

Behind much of the public fascination with the Amish story at Nickel Mines is the mirror that their actions held up to each one of us: what would I have done in such a circumstance? Even if I thought that forgiveness was the appropriate Christian response, would I honestly have had the inner strength to take that path? What would it take for "ordinary" people like you and me to become this virtuous?

Most people, regardless of religious background, believe that living virtuously is a good thing. All parents want their children to be trustworthy and honest. Politicians of all stripes agree that public servants should be people of integrity. Today, virtually every professional school in the country requires its students—budding lawyers, doctors, accountants, and CEOs—to take at least one class in "professional ethics" in the hopes that graduates will behave ethically. Yet very few groups can claim a high degree of success. So, what was the secret behind the Amish response?

The answer may well lie in our assumptions about the formation of Christian character. Many of us take it for granted that the key to virtuous behavior—or ethics—is education. We assume that people become virtuous by thinking carefully about their actions and then acting accordingly. Socrates once said, "To know the Good is to will the Good," by which he meant that once we understand rationally what the "right" decision should be in a given circumstance, we will naturally be inclined to follow through in a virtuous way. If, for example, the criminal can come to recognize that the long-term consequences of stealing are harmful even to himself, then he will quit acting foolishly and make better choices in the future. Being a good person, therefore, requires us to reflect carefully on the consequences of our choices, make a judgment on the basis of some principle (usually something like "the greatest good for the greatest number of people") and then to act appropriately.

A long tradition of Christian ethics has borrowed heavily from these basic assumptions. Although some Christians may claim that ethics is simply a matter of obeying your conscience or asking "what would Jesus do?" in reality we generally pursue some variation of the more standard approach. We recognize that the world is full of ethical gray areas where we are forced to choose between competing ideals—for example, Christ's call to love enemies versus the Christian responsibility to defend the weak. The first step, then, is to analyze the dilemma by breaking it down logically into its various parts; then we apply some general principle (perhaps the Golden Rule) to determine the "correct" response. Then we follow through with the appropriate behavior.

In theory, this approach to Christian ethics seems to make sense. In actual practice, however, its limitations quickly become clear. When confronted with a moral choice, few of us are apt to actually step back, consider all the relevant biblical teachings, apply some larger principle, and then move to a deliberate, carefully nuanced decision. In reality, almost all of our moral decisions are made "on the fly" in the heat of the moment. We might reflect critically on our decision afterward, but each time the sales clerk overlooks an item in our shopping cart or mistakenly hands us a twenty rather a ten-dollar bill in change, we don't call for a time-out to sort through the high-minded principles involved in our response.

Moreover, anyone who has struggled with an addiction or the simple reality of our sinful nature recognizes that Socrates' claim that "knowing the good" will inevitably lead us to "will the good" is just plain wrong. Knowing what we *should* do is no guarantee of what we *will* do. In fact, we frequently make bad moral choices not because we are ignorant but because our desire to act on impulse simply outweighs our desire to be good. As the apostle Paul lamented, all too often we fail to do precisely those things that we know we should do (see Romans 7:19).

Finally, when we talk about ethical choices in this manner, we tend to focus on dilemmas that seemingly force us to make tragic compromises between "ideals" and "reality." Yet these apparent dilemmas may actually only be a sign of an immature faith. Of course there are moments when we need to make decisions based on inadequate information, under time constraints, and without any certainty of the outcome. But we should hesitate before too quickly declaring that all difficult moral decisions are "gray areas" in which—tragically—compromises must be made.

Here is only one example: Most Christians throughout history have insisted that under certain circumstances, it is legitimate for Christians to kill other human beings. But the arguments defending "just war" rest on a logic that *anyone* could make, regardless of whether or not you happen to be a Christian. It is quite possible that in our defense of the gray-area circumstances that bless Christian participation in lethal violence, we are actually forfeiting an opportunity to bear witness to our hope in the resurrection—our confidence that life in Christ will triumph over the forces of death. After all, Christ's own decision to confront the power of evil did not end in the tragedy of the cross but in the resurrection and the ultimate victory of life over death. When the ethical choices we confront seemingly lock us into a corner where some compromise with violence or evil is the only way out, Christians can still make choices—perhaps sacrificially—that affirm the power of Christ's transforming love.

None of this suggests that careful thinking about ethics is a waste of time, or that "true Christians" will always know precisely the nature of God's will in every situation, or that we will always possess the maturity of moral character to do the right thing. But we are misguided to think that we will be transformed into virtuous Christians primarily by becoming more sophisticated in our ethical reasoning.

How, then, do Christians become more Christlike? The solution in the Christian tradition is both remarkably simple and profoundly challenging.

Practices: Character Formation in the Context of Community

The simple response to this profound challenge can be easily summarized: Christians become virtuous by worshipping regularly together in communities whose practices bear witness to the incarnation of Christ.

What do I mean by that? Here the example of the Amish response to the Nickel Mines massacre can be helpful. Some commentators, used to thinking about ethics as a series of rational choices made by each individual, criticized the Amish impulse to forgive as the result of "group think"—the outcome of socialization so powerful that it bordered on the coercive. What these critics overlooked, however, is the fact that our ethical choices reflect our *character* more than our ability to engage in complex ethical reasoning. By character, I mean our engrained habits, dispositions, and assumptions, formed over time in the context of a community, that express our deepest understanding of how the world works.

Thinkers as far back as Aristotle have recognized that ethical behavior is shaped more profoundly by the communities that nurture us than by a rational decision-making process or a heroic exercise of the will. Individual reflection on our choices is not irrelevant to ethical behavior, but becoming a virtuous person is more a matter of repeated practice in doing the right thing within the context of a well-defined community than it is becoming skillful in ethical reasoning. In short, character, not the intellect, is at the heart of virtue.

In recent decades, various philosophers, ethicists, and theologians have found it helpful to think about the process of character formation in terms of *practices*. The concept of practices is useful because it holds together a number of different themes often treated in isolation from each other or even regarded as incompatible. In our ordinary use of the term we might think of practices as (1) *actions that are customary and seemingly routine but still done with intentionality*. A handshake, for example, is a common practice that we do without much thought. Yet we are also at least vaguely aware of a larger purpose behind the action: a ready handshake is a gesture of familiarity and friendship. Beyond that—though we almost never think about it in this way—a handshake also signals our desire to relate to each other peacefully by making it clear that we are not carrying a weapon in our right hand.

A somewhat deeper meaning suggested by practices is (2) *the conscious, disciplined training necessary to achieve some larger purpose or good.* If you want to become a proficient guitar player, you will need to practice simple chords over and over, with the goal of eventually moving into more complex chords that you can play without thinking about where to place your fingers on the fret board. Playing a chord correctly is the immediate goal of practice—and a source of some pleasure if you get it right. But the point of these repeated exercises is understood best within the context of a larger good—namely, to play with such (seemingly) effortless skill that all the hours of practice are nearly forgotten in the sheer beauty of the music.

There is yet a third related understanding of practices that adds still another important dimension. If we say that somebody practices law or medicine we are assuming (3) *a set of skills, behaviors, or qualities associated with a profession.* In this sense, a doctor is not merely engaging in a series of isolated activities; she is participating in a medical practice that has a deep history and tradition, with standards for membership, a code of conduct, internal forms of discipline, all directed toward a larger, overarching purpose. If a doctor is truly skillful, the routine practices of the first meaning (such as taking blood pressure) become the basis for a skilled diagnosis, pointing to the second meaning. Both of these are absolutely necessary to be a good physician. But the good inherent to a medical practice—the health and well-being of the patient—ultimately cannot be reduced to accurate blood-pressure readings or a prescription for hypertension. A good medical practice becomes so only within the context of many diagnoses across a long period of time that are informed and reinforced by the community of medical practitioners who are consciously representing the long tradition of their profession.

It may be helpful to consider another example. When I first tried to learn Spanish, I bought a dozen books on "how to learn Spanish," resolved to learn five new words a day, and made lists of verbs to memorize. After several weeks, I discovered that even though I spent hours studying verb conjugations and the rules of pronunciation, if I was ever going to become proficient I would need to practice actually speaking the language. I might know a lot of vocabulary words, but fluency required meaningful application in a community of native Spanish speakers.

My approach to language learning changed dramatically when our family moved to Costa Rica for a year to direct a service-learning program and I was forced to speak Spanish every day. Initially, the process was highly self-conscious; each sentence was a laborious construction, and at the end of the day, I often felt exhausted, confused, and full of self-doubt. But slowly, almost imperceptibly, certain sentences begin to fall into place. Gradually, I realized that I was able to converse sufficiently to meet with host families, organize lectures, plan bus excursions, establish service placements, handle financial transactions, and respond to minor crises. Both types of practices—memorization of words and a task-oriented level of fluency—were clearly helping me toward the goal of learning Spanish.

However, it wasn't until I began to develop friendships with Costa Ricans that language acquisition took on yet another, even deeper meaning. At some point, I realized that the true end or purpose of my efforts was not to "learn Spanish" but to enter into trusting and intimate relationships with people who happened to speak a different language. This implied a willingness to submit to the rules of grammar and an openness to be corrected on a regular basis. But mastering the language was not in itself the primary good. Once my focus began to shift from linguistic mastery to relationships, the nature of my study began to change, and a different kind of fluency began to emerge. Learning Spanish became far less of a struggle and much more joyful. I began to let go of the classroom goal of grammatical perfection and to communicate from the heart. I did not live in Costa Rica long enough to become fully fluent. But I noticed somewhere along the way that as I entered into the surprising intricacies of cross-cultural relationships, the practice of learning a language was helping me to become a different person.

Worship Practices as Christian Formation: Yielding to God in *Gelassenheit*

Every analogy has its limitations. I do not mean here to reduce growth in Christian virtue—what is sometimes called *sanctification*—to a simple, three-step formula. But the concept of practices does offer a helpful framework for thinking about how the regular habits of worship find expression in daily life.

Here again, the Amish response at Nickel Mines is instructive. One thing that impressed outsiders was how quickly the members of the Amish community expressed their forgiveness to the family of the murderer. Clearly, the Amish did not need to form an ethics committee or spend long hours in careful theological deliberation about whether forgiveness was the appropriate response. Their reaction was immediate, genuine, and seemingly unanimous. When pressed about this point, the Amish responded with bewilderment. Indeed, in conversations with reporters in the weeks that followed the shootings, they insisted that the forgiveness extended to the Robert's family was not extraordinary.

Many mentioned the fact that at least twice a day and at every worship service they recite together the Lord's Prayer, in which they ask God to forgive their sins by the same standard that "we forgive those who sin against us." The words are so simple. Yet they make a stunning claim: God's free and gracious forgiveness of us cannot ultimately be separated from the way we forgive others, including—perhaps *especially* including—our enemies. What made their response unheroic is the fact that this prayer and the larger theme of forgiveness is so central to the practices of being Amish. The language of forgiveness permeates Amish hymns and prayers. Stories of forgiveness are a standard part of Amish oral tradition. In fact, reporters covering the Nickel Mines story soon began to uncover dozens of other, far less publicized cases in which the Amish forgave offenders or befriended the families of those who had done them harm.

Forgiveness at Nickel Mines, therefore, was not a heroic human achievement but a natural reaction, rooted in daily reminders of the boundless and unmerited love of God, expressed in regular practices of giving and receiving forgiveness. In this context, forgiveness in a time of crisis seemed self-evident.

Crucial in all of this is the fact that these practices had been nurtured within a broader community. Because the Amish way of life is so strongly oriented to the larger group, some critics have suggested that they are caught up in a self-centered form of "works righteousness." That concern raises deeper questions about the ultimate end to which the practices of the Amish community are directed—what philosophers sometimes call the *telos* of the community. Is the goal of these practices simply group conformity, or are they directed to some other higher purpose?

The Amish tend not to be highly explicit or self-conscious about the rationale behind every aspect of their life. If you ask Amish people to explain a particular practice, they may refer to tradition more than to a specific Scripture verse. And because they almost never talk about spirituality—the individualistic and emotion-laden language of a "personal relationship with God"—it could seem as if the work of the Spirit is not central to their way of life. But if you spend any amount of time in Amish circles, you quickly become aware that their lives, and the very structure of their community, is indeed shaped by a deep spirituality.

At the heart of Amish spirituality is the practice of *Gelassenheit,* or "yieldedness." In its simplest form, *Gelassenheit* (*uffgevva* in Pennsylvania Dutch) is a posture of Christian humility, a way of being in the world in which the self is yielded to God in every aspect of life. Gelassenheit is cultivated in the daily practices of prayer, mutual accountability, and a willing vulnerability to each other and to God. It finds expression in such diverse areas of Amish life as speech patterns, dress style, body posture, occupational choices, child rearing, and decision making. Gelassenheit is at the core of the early Christian hymn that Paul quotes in Philippians when he describes the willing self-emptying of Christ:

> Do nothing out of selfish ambition or vain conceit, but in humility consider others better than yourselves. Each of

you should look not only to your own interests, but also to the interests of others. Your attitude should be the same as that of Christ Jesus: who, being in very nature God, did not consider equality with God something to be grasped, but made himself nothing, taking the very nature of a servant, being made in human likeness. And being found in appearance as a man, he humbled himself and became obedient to death—even death on a cross! (Philippians 2:3-8)

To be sure, the Amish take the teachings of Jesus very seriously. "If anyone loves me, he will obey my teaching," Jesus said (John 14: 23). But the larger goal of the community is not to mechanically reproduce the teachings of Christ in a dogged form of works righteousness. Rather, Amish practices are intended to help believers yield themselves to the Spirit of God—which is the true purpose of the Christian community.

Obedience to Christ's teachings assumes that the Christian is "made new in the attitude of your minds" and has "put on the new self, created to be like God in true righteousness and holiness" (Ephesians 4:23-24). Thus, one recurring image in many Anabaptist and Amish writings is the gospel metaphor of a branch connected to the vine. "I am the vine, you are the branches," Jesus instructed his disciples. "Those who abide in me and I in them bear much fruit, because apart from me you can do nothing. . . . If you abide in me, and my words abide in you, ask for whatever you wish, and it will be done for you" (John 15:5, 7 NRSV). The branch is completely dependent on the vine for its life, but the evidence that the branch is indeed alive is found in the fruit that it bears. Life in the vine will inevitably produce fruit; otherwise, one can assume that the branch is dead. This same image is repeated in Galatians with reference to the work of the Holy Spirit made visible in the fruits of the Spirit: love, joy, peace, patience, kindness, goodness, faithfulness, gentleness, self-control (see Galatians 5:22-23).

Gelassenheit also assumes that participation in the vine of Christ includes the possibility of sharing in Christ's suffering. In the garden of Gethsemane, Jesus demonstrated Gelassenheit in his anguished prayer asking God to "take this cup from me," a prayer that concluded nonetheless with the words "not my will, but yours be done" (Luke 22:42). Suffering is never a goal to be sought; it is simply a likely outcome if one is truly yielded to Christ. Thus Paul writes, "I have been crucified with Christ and I no longer live, but Christ lives in me. The life I live in the body, I live by faith in the Son of God, who loved me and gave himself for me" (Galatians 2:20).

Overarching all these distinctive practices in the Amish community is a profound sense that every aspect of life is an expression of Christian faith. Theirs is not a "Sunday morning" faith disconnected from how one dresses, speaks, acts, or lives during the rest of the week. Although the Amish themselves would not use the term, they have a *sacramental* understanding of life that regards everything they do as an expression of worship and, in a similar way, everything they do as a Christian witness. All of life has the potential of being transformed into an expression of worship; all of life has the potential of bearing witness to the nature of the God whom we serve.

Why Do Practices Matter?

In the chapters thus far, I have attempted to present the basic components of salvation from an Anabaptist-Mennonite perspective. We began with the incarnation: a view of the world in which all creation is latent with the presence of God's glory, expressed in its most dramatic and profound form in the person of Jesus Christ. In Jesus, the Word was made flesh, and in Christ, we have the possibility of being reconciled to God and with each other. The full meaning of the incarnation is known to us first in worship—gathering with other Christians to offer praise, to declare our allegiances, to see the world truthfully, and to embody the presence of the resurrected Christ in our time and place in the life of the church.

Finally, in this chapter, I have suggested that our ethical behavior is shaped less by a process of careful reflection and conscious act of the will than it is by the communities around us. If you want to be a virtuous Christian who puts faith into action, you will need to develop the habits and dispositions of a virtuous person. That will require lots of practice in the context of a nurturing community whose entire worldview is directed toward worshipping God. If the incarnation is true, then the habits of worship, nurtured in the Christian community, will inevitably take on visible form: to participate in Christ is to share not only in his spirit but also in his body.

If this approach to Christian ethics, rooted in the practices of worship, makes sense, then how can it become relevant for the church today? In some ways, the answer to that question is the focus of the rest of the book. For now, though, I offer two brief suggestions.

1. Worship practices transform us into new creatures in Christ. Anchoring ethics in the context of Christian practices and the deeper foundation of the incarnation and worship may help contemporary Mennonites avoid two opposing tendencies that are needlessly dividing the church today. One tendency among some missions-minded Mennonites is to imagine Christian faith almost exclusively in terms of a personal relationship with Jesus. In this understanding, salvation is a kind of inner on/off switch that gets turned on at the moment one makes a public confession of faith in Christ.

In terms of missions strategies, this approach tends to focus on the persuasive language or tactics necessary to get the sinner to say "yes" to Christ. Once that happens and the switch is flipped, everything else in the Christian journey becomes of secondary importance, mere accessories of doctrine or tradition or ethical practices that are not really very important in comparison to the more significant fact that you have been "saved." Thus Mennonite congregations operating in this mode are tempted to withhold information regarding distinctive Anabaptist-Mennonite teachings on nonresistance or mutual accountability or other ethical practices, fearing that these would be unnecessary obstacles to potential newcomers. The church should simply preach "salvation" and let each individual sort out how they want to apply the gospel in the privacy of their own lives.

A second, equally problematic tendency in other Mennonite churches is to define salvation primary in terms of following the teachings of Jesus. Here Christian faith can easily be reduced to a short list of "peace and justice" issues often defined in terms of specific political policies, which then become the litmus test for authentic discipleship. Yet this approach turns out to be merely another variation of the on/off switch. Once a person is committed to fighting the injustices of the world, all other considerations of the Christian faith—perhaps especially those related to worship, prayer, or doctrine—become secondary, mere accessories to the more important fact that you are working for the cause of peace. As long as newcomers to the church are committed to "peace and justice," they are free to believe whatever they wish—or even to have no particular religious commitments at all.

A view of Christian practices anchored in the incarnation and worship suggests that both of these tendencies are fundamentally misguided. Each is a modern variation on the heresies of the early church: whereas the first elevates Jesus to a disembodied Cosmic Savior in the docetist tradition, the second reduces him into an Exemplary Teacher, usually modeled after our own image.

At its best, the Anabaptist-Mennonite tradition has understood salvation in richer, more complex, and more dynamic terms. Salvation begins with a recognition of our human shortcomings and a desire for repentance. Saying yes to God's gracious offer of forgiveness is a crucial step in that process. But salvation cannot be rightly understood apart from true conversion, that is, a qualitative change of character, made possible by the empowering grace of God, which becomes evident in concrete behavior.

In numerous interrogation records, Anabaptists reported that they joined the movement because of "powerful preaching" that called them to repent from sin, to yield themselves fully to the Spirit, to be baptized into the new community of faith, to study Scripture, and to live a life modeled after that of Christ.[5] Salvation pointed toward the transformation of the believer into a "new creation in Christ" (2 Corinthians 5:17). The new Christian was transformed not only by the inner work of God's forgiving grace but also by an outward change in daily behavior made possible by God's empowering grace.

There are many ways to talk about this, but Paul's familiar words in Ephesians capture the point eloquently: "For it is by grace that you have been saved, through faith—and this not from yourselves, it is the gift of God—not by your works, so that no one can boast" (2:8-9). This classic text of the Protestant Reformation is one that Anabaptist groups like the Amish and the Mennonites have always embraced. We will not close the gap between humanity and God by our own efforts—not by right emotions, right doctrines, right behaviors, or even the right worship practices. Rather, God loved us preemptively, "while we were still sinners" (Romans 5:8). So everything that follows is a response to God's invitation.

Yet salvation does not end there. To assume, as some Christians seem to do, that Christian faith is only about receiving God's gift of grace is like confusing a wedding with a marriage. A wedding sets the context for a marriage in the sense that everything that follows unfolds against the backdrop of its blessing, a blessing renewed every day. But the whole point of the wedding—the thing that makes it a gift—is the adventure and excitement of the lifelong relationship that follows. This is why early Anabaptists insisted that the familiar verse from Ephesians 2:9 regarding our salvation "by grace alone" also be read in association with the verse that immediately follows it: "For we are God's workmanship, *created in Christ Jesus to do good works*, which God prepared in advance for us to do" (verse 10, emphasis added).

The move from grace to good works here is not an afterthought or an add-on. Good works are not simply an "accessory" to salvation that one can take or leave. They are the inevitable outcome of our salvation by grace. Indeed, if our life in Christ is *not* made visible in good works, then God's "workmanship" will not be evident in our lives, and we will be living contrary to that which "God prepared in advance for us to do."

The routine practices of worship should remind us that Christian faith begins with God's initiative of grace and our *yes* to that invitation. Our identity within the body of Christ is first and foremost a consequence of God's action and not something that we have to negotiate. Yet God's presence is never an abstraction. It is always made visible, however obscurely or imperfectly, in worship practices that form our character into the likeness of Christ. Paul suggests in 2 Corinthians that we become what we gaze at: "We all, with unveiled face, beholding as in a mirror the glory of the Lord, are being transformed into the same image from glory to glory" (2 Corinthians 3:18 NKJV).

If we are going to be transformed into the glory of the Lord, it will begin by practices rehearsed in the church—not an abstract or theoretical church, but the local congregation made up of real people. After all, we don't learn how to speak Spanish in some vague place like Latin America. We learn it in Barcelona or Alejuela, and ultimately in a specific barrio, from real people with whom we eat together, laugh together, and work together. Proficiency in Spanish is never reducible to the place where you learned the language; but you can become proficient only by immersion "on the ground."

Practices of worship renew us in the grace of God, while also transforming us into people who are prepared to embody that grace in virtuous lives.

2. Worship practices inevitably spill out beyond the church: sharing the abundance. There is a second important characteristic of worship practices, one that I will only introduce here since it will be the primary focus of the chapters that follow. For many modern people, the division between the private world of faith and the public world of everyday life is clear: if the church has a place in their lives at all, it will be kept separate from other aspects of life.

For the Christian shaped by worship, however, this distinction makes no sense. Because worship is rooted in the abundance of God's love, which exceeds anything we are able to imagine or grasp or contain, this love will inevitably extend beyond the church to the world around. Indeed, God's presence becomes real and tangible—the gospel truly becomes good news—only when it spills out beyond ourselves and is shared with those around. As worship practices transform the actions and attitudes of believers the gospel is made visible to the world: the practices of worship are inevitably *missional.*

Consider several examples. As I have noted, some Mennonites today have come to think of the Anabaptist-Mennonite peace witness as an impediment to missions. Yet this hesitancy to link salvation to reconciliation with enemies misses an essential part of the gospel. As a Christian, I do not teach my children to love their enemies because it's heroic or because I'm a Mennonite or because I'm a liberal. Rather, I hope that they will love their enemies simply because that is exactly what God did for us. God loved us even though we did not deserve it. Christians testify to the depths of God's unconditional love for the world only when they are prepared to love other people in the same way God does—sacrificially and unconditionally. Loving enemies, letting go of resentments, or offering forgiveness instead of retaliation are not "Mennonite" doctrines. They are the natural and inevitable response of those who have received this same kind of love from God. Loving enemies is simply part of the good news of the gospel.

In a similar way, Christians who are formed by the practices of worship will not hesitate to speak the truth in public settings in ways that sometimes are offensive to cultural norms. Because the gospel frees us to live open, transparent, and truthful lives, Christians cannot help but challenge the falsehoods and lies of the society in which we live. Thus when Christians call friends to account who are hiding their loneliness with alcohol, drugs, computer games, or a long string of sexual conquests; or when Christians speak out against racism or gender inequality in the local community; or when Christians publicly lament that we spend more than one billion dollars a day on armaments while thirty-five thousand people around the world die daily from starvation, they are not simply being snobbish critics of their society. Rather, they are naming the lies from which the world needs to be saved. Telling the truth is part of the good news of the gospel.

To be sure, telling the truth does not always feel like good news. The practice of truth-telling often challenges cherished assumptions; it may threaten the status quo or name our deepest fears. And sometimes Christians trying to speak the truth about the world forget that God actually loves the world, even in its brokenness. But telling the gospel truth is indeed good news. "You will know the truth," Jesus promised, "and the truth will set you free" (John 8:32).

Finally, worship spills over into the world around—worship

becomes missional—when Christians actively participate with God in ministries of healing and reconciliation. Indeed, Christians cannot fully experience the power of God's healing in their own lives until they are prepared to offer themselves in the healing of others. Christian worship practices will inevitably call us into the world to share in God's healing work. Acts of charity, service, and compassion are nothing more than the public expression of the good news of the gospel: if one side of the coin is what God has done for us, the other side must be the reality of God's love, truth, and healing extended into the world. Christians extend the sacrament of peace when they participate with God in the healing of the world's brokenness.

The larger point here should be clear. Worship names the good news that we have received; yet we have not truly received the gospel unless we become the means through which that good news is incarnated in the world as a witness to God's loving and healing presence.

Conclusion: Worship and Witness Are Inseparable

When my student sheepishly acknowledged that he had not been attending church, even though he considered himself to be a Christian, he was accurately reflecting an attitude shared by many others. For many young people today, the church seems like an old and tired institution kept alive by sheer inertia and the memories of its own traditions. Faced with shrinking memberships, congregations are often tempted to respond to these criticisms by assuming that tradition is the problem and marketing is the solution. Since the free market puts a premium on individual choice, a consumer-centered response starts by testing market demand and then creates a product that will guarantee customer satisfaction.

If the argument I have suggested above regarding Christian practices is correct, however, we should think twice about this logic. The problem is not with the desire to be relevant. If the church is going to grow, it needs to be addressing questions that people are actually asking. Yet the true relevance of the church is not determined by market studies but by addressing more seriously the ethics gap that characterizes much of modern Christianity. When our professed beliefs do not align with our actions, people have a right to be skeptical about the urgency and authority of the truth we are offering.

The key question for church growth, then, is less a matter of Christian doctrine than it is of Christian practices—formative practices shaped by a worshipping community that spill out of the congregation to find expression in the ordinary flow of daily life.

If my student was genuinely interested in an argument for regular church attendance, I would start by asking him what community is currently shaping his character. The first step to recovering the relevance of the church is to help those outside the church recognize that they have not ceased to worship simply because they quit attending church. Even if my student may not acknowledge the fact, his ethical choices are always being shaped by the practices of a community—if not the church then some other community. What company is he keeping? Who are the people he cares most about in terms of approval and acceptance? What is the telos—the end to which that community is devoted? Faith will always find expression in the material; the spirit will always be incarnated. Your deepest convictions are always finding expression in specific and concrete ways. In this sense, the claim to be "spiritual but not religious" is simply an impossibility.

Second, I would suggest to my student that the community gathered in Christ's name offers a powerful understanding of the human condition, a highly relevant critique of the cultural currents of our day, and a true account of the possibility of being genuinely reconciled with each other, with creation, and with God. That story is told and embodied in the community of people who gather regularly for worship. To participate in that community is to witness the incarnation of God—the Word made flesh. The practices of that community offer genuine healing of mind, body, and spirit.

To a mass and impersonal culture, the good news of the gospel is that the word was made flesh in the person of Jesus Christ. Faith is not an abstraction, technique, or gimmick but a new way of life made real in the concrete practices of the body of Christ.

To an individualistic culture, the good news of the gospel is that you are not alone. You can become part of a story as old as creation itself—a story of a God who has acted in history, a God who knows your name and invites you to become part of this story. To participate in the story is to join a community of people who love you and care for you, who laugh and cry with you, who challenge you to exercise your gifts and call you to account when you fail.

To a culture addicted to consumerism, the good news of the gospel is that you can be freed from the burden of possessions. You can discover the beauty of a simple life. You can find liberation from grasping onto material things, knowing that the "earth is the Lord's" (Psalm 24:1) and that we are only stewards of creation.

In the end, though, the strongest argument I could make to my student is not one that will convince him logically but rather an invitation to come back to church and to participate fully in the practices of worship. Of course, the congregation he visits has to be a true community. The members of the church need to have some intentionality about their worship. Their worship must be informing their lives in ways that are visible. Above all, there must be a deep sense of joy in their worship and witness. Paul captures this point well when he prays that the church in Ephesus will "have power . . . to grasp how wide and long and high and deep is the love of Christ, and to know this love that surpasses knowledge" (Ephesians 3:18-19).

We were created by God for intimacy, authentic lives of trust, generosity, and love. By practicing the presence of God in worship we can experience true reconciliation with God, with each other and with creation. And this is good news!

Part 2

Witness

5

Bearing Witness in Our Bodies

One morning several years ago, an unusual pain in my chest launched a series of events that led my doctor to think that I was in the midst of a heart attack. Fortunately, he was wrong. Today my heart seems to be as healthy as can be expected for a person my age. But during the course of that strange day I got a chance to see something I had never seen before.

Shortly after I arrived by ambulance at the local hospital, a technician wheeled a large machine into my room that was connected to a TV monitor. As she pressed a medical instrument to my chest, I suddenly saw on the screen the shadowy image of my own heart steadily beating.

To be sure, it wasn't a very clear picture. She had to point out to me the exact location of various arteries and valves. But it was unmistakably a beating heart. And what's more, it was my heart that was there beating on the screen! As I watched its rhythmic, steady twitching and thumping, I was filled with a sense of wonder and awe. Here was the engine of my earthly existence hard at work, steadily pumping, day in and day out, 365 days a year. While I worked, rested, exercised, or did nothing at all, it was quietly going about its job of keeping me alive. Yet most of the time—in fact, almost all the time—I wasn't even aware of it.

The experience left me with two rather intense realizations that have stayed with me ever since. The first was a recognition that we cannot ignore the basic mechanics of our bodies. Our physical, flesh-and-blood bodies come with no guarantees. Even though my illness turned out to be a false alarm, I left the hospital the next day with a new sense of the fragility of my body and a sobering reminder that someday my heart is going to stop beating.

The second lingering memory from that ordeal was the sheer wonder of life itself. What an astounding thing it is to be alive! Watching the shadowy image of my own beating heart left me amazed once again by the pulsing, vibrant miracle of life—a miracle that could never be reduced to the sum of medical facts about the physical condition of my body.

So we live with a paradox. We are bodies, yet who we are always exceeds the physical. We are alive, yet our awareness of the sheer wonder of life cannot be known apart from the biochemistry of our physical bodies.

At the heart of this mystery is an echo of the incarnation. We are *living sacraments*—physical beings created in the image of God. Yet the Spirit of God that gives us life can never be reduced to our physical self. We are ensouled bodies and embodied souls.

In the previous chapter, I suggested that worship is not merely a spiritual bridge between humans and God. Rather, through the power of the Holy Spirit, our participation in the practices of worship shapes us into the likeness of Christ. This chapter begins an exploration of how the communion with God and with each other that we normally associate with Sunday morning spills out beyond the confines of church into the more routine, public world of our everyday life. In the following chapters, we will look at how worship leads to witness in four different contexts: our bodies, our families, the public world of our communities, and the physical spaces of our worship.

Describing the Christian witness to the world in these categories has some drawbacks, especially since it seems to impose artificial distinctions between our bodies and our families, or our families and communities. Clearly, our bodies accompany us in every aspect of life; and we don't cease to be family members when we bear witness to our faith in the community. At our best, *all* of life is worship and *all* of life is a celebration of the reconciliation and wholeness made possible by the incarnation of Jesus Christ. Nonetheless, these distinction are a useful way of bringing sharper focus and clarity to the varied expressions of Christian witness in the world. My intention in what follows is to sketch a few key areas where these practices of worship find expression in witness.

Cultural Confusion About Our Bodies

The Christian tradition has sometimes offered mixed messages about our bodies. One reading of the New Testament would seem to suggest that the physical body is an enemy of the true Christian. We can readily identify with the lament that "the spirit is willing, but the body is weak" (Matthew 26:41). The apostle Paul supposedly hated the body, regarding it as fallen, prone to sin and locked into a ceaseless battle with the Spirit. Various New Testament texts speak of an ongoing battle against the lusts and the desires of the flesh (see Romans 8:5-13; Galatians 5:16-17), or compare our earthly bodies in a negative way to our heavenly bodies (see 1 Corinthians 5:42-43).

One explanation for this seemingly negative attitude is the fact that, unlike our spirit, our body is corruptible; it is in a steady process of decay and wearing out. Inevitably our physical bodies will come face to face with death. For some early Christians, the conclusion was obvious: since our bodies change and will eventually die, they must be inferior to the soul that gives us life.

In medieval Catholicism, these concerns gave rise to the ascetic tradition of "mortifying the flesh." If the spirit was the source of life and the body an enemy of the soul, then the body would need to be disciplined by practices like extended fasts, wearing uncomfortable clothing, or a commitment to celibacy. Our souls, some church fathers taught, can be properly nourished only by keeping the body under tight control.

Few Christians today are inclined to defend this logic. Indeed, contemporary Christians are much more likely to join with the broader culture in a general celebration of the body. We are immersed daily in thousands of images of the human form in all its visual variety. Our cultural obsession with sports is driven, in part, by our desire to see bodies in action and to celebrate the potential of the human physique by pushing bodies to their very limits. We are deeply fascinated with the physical mechanics of the human form. Television crime dramas have become increasingly explicit in their depictions of bodily trauma and violent deaths. They offer us lingering and explicit camera shots of autopsies in morgues or bodies in various stages of physical decomposition. The popular "Body Exhibit," which drew more than a million spectators across the nation, literally pulls back the skin of actual human bodies to reveal the muscles, nerves, and bones beneath, while other displays provide graphic views of bodies sliced up in dozens of cross-sections. In these and many other ways, one could argue that our culture embraces and celebrates the body in all its physical forms.

Yet beneath this apparent public affirmation of the body is a much more complicated reality. Behind our obsession with the physical body, a host of confusing and contradictory assumptions reveal a deep estrangement from our physical selves. Indeed, it is not exaggerating to say that we are actually a culture at war with our bodies. This is a bold claim. But consider the following tensions focused on our bodies that seem to be prevalent in modern life.

1. Food. No bodily function is more basic to our survival than our physical appetite, our hunger for food. We must eat to live. Throughout history, Christians have always regarded food as a sign of God's blessing and abundance. When we pray "give us this day our daily bread," we acknowledge that our very existence depends on food. In a world where thirty-five thousand people die each day from hunger-related causes, we should never take that prayer for granted.

At the same time, however, we also know that eating is about much more than caloric intake for our physical survival. If we ate only when we were actually hungry, we would eat far less than we do. Instead, we eat out of habit. We eat to divert ourselves from boredom or fear. We eat for the pleasure of savoring flavors in our mouths. We eat "comfort food" when we are anxious or sick. We eat because powerful commercials play hidden messages in our minds, telling us that particular foods will make us healthier, happier, more popular, or more attractive.

Because appetite and consumption are rarely in harmony with our actual physical needs, our society is facing a growing epidemic of obesity and weight-related diseases. Our obsession with food has created a thousand different diets, given rise to a growing number of eating disorders, and spawned whole industries in exercise equipment, vitamins, and food supplements. We love to eat, but we end up hating the bodies that result from our overconsumption.

2. Beauty. In a related way, consider our cultural obsession with the shape and proportion of the human body. All of us yearn for beauty. We deeply desire to be attractive in ways that will make others take note of us and want to be in our presence. Our hunger for physical beauty is profound. Yet our categories and vocabulary for describing beauty remain remarkably underdeveloped. Since bodies are the most tangible forms of our identity, our culture frequently defines beauty by an extremely narrow—often elusive—ideal of the perfect body form, usually with exaggerated attention to sexuality. To be beautiful is to be young, trim, and sexy. As the raw material out of which beauty must be crafted, our bodies must be sliced and shaped, nipped and tucked, exercised, dieted, and disciplined in order to approximate those ideal standards.

Yet physical beauty is always temporary. Fashions change, wrinkles appear, gravity and aging eventually compel our bodies to sag, and no amount of Botox injections, collagen implants, or plastic surgery can ever change these fundamental realities.

So once again we end up at war with our bodies. We yearn for physical beauty, but the ideal for which we strive is always beyond our ability to reach or maintain.

3. Intimacy. Behind the quest for beauty is an even deeper hunger for intimacy. God created us to live with each other in openness and transparency. We have an innate desire to be connected with those around us, to reveal our full selves—our hopes, our fears, our strengths, and our weaknesses—in the confidence that others will not use our self-revelation for their own gain.

All too often, however, our culture reduces this deep craving for human intimacy to the physical act of sex. That God designed us as sexual beings is undoubtedly a gift worthy of thanksgiving. Sexual intercourse is a blessing precisely because it can be an expression of true intimacy, anchored in a marriage covenant of enduring trust and commitment that is ultimately rooted in God's unconditional love.

Yet the physical pleasure of sex is always fleeting. It points us to the deep human hunger to participate in the incarnation—a moment when time and eternity seem to intersect—but that moment never lasts.

The irony of our highly sexualized culture is that physical intimacy apart from a covenant of trust and commitment inevitably leaves one feeling even more isolated and lonely than before. Faced with failure in the quest for intimacy, many are tempted to numb the pain of loneliness with alcohol or medications or to desperately pursue alternative forms of ecstasy in drugs, pornography, or serial sexual relations. Or perhaps we simply retreat into the disembodied, virtual intimacy of internet relationships in which we reveal carefully selected parts of ourselves without ever needing to encounter others in our actual bodies.

Once again, our bodies let us down. We crave vulnerability and intimacy, yet our physical bodies seem to become an obstacle to the very thing they crave.

4. Death. At the root of these yearnings lies the deepest human desire of all: to cheat death and live forever. When Adam and Eve ate of the fruit of the garden, they did so hoping that, like God, they would be immortal. That hunger for life is in itself surely no sin. After all, the Bible is filled with references to the goodness of life as a precious gift. Yet once again, our culture often reduces this God-given affirmation of life to a very narrow focus on our physical bodies. As a result, we spend billions of dollars prolonging our youth, fighting the signs of aging, and doing "whatever it takes" to postpone death, regardless of the costs. Recent estimates suggest that more than half of all healthcare costs are spent during the last two months of life, desperately trying to ward off the inevitable.

Because we know that our bodies are running down—that even now, cancer cells may be lurking unnoticed, waiting for the call to action—we hunger, sometimes desperately, for recognition and fame. If we can't live forever, we at least want to be noticed, even for only fifteen minutes of fame.

Here, too, however, our bodies disappoint us. Physical death may be postponed, but it is never preventable. Our time on earth is transitory; we will all die, celebrities will be forgotten, and our gravestones will eventually become illegible.

So we seem to be locked in a ceaseless and confusing struggle. We celebrate our bodies, but we are also haunted by an even deeper awareness that our bodies confront us with problems so basic we can scarcely name them. They are the empty houses of our loneliness, the embodied form of our alienation from each other and from God.

In the face of so much confusion, does the gospel offer any good news about our bodies? What would a Christian witness to the world look like if it was expressed in our bodies? Is there anything distinctive that the Anabaptist-Mennonite tradition has to offer in the quest for a healthy understanding of our bodies?

Bearing Witness to the Incarnation in Our Bodies

"Do you not know that your body is a temple of the Holy Spirit, who is in you, whom you have received from God? You are not your own; you were bought at a price. Therefore honor God with your body" (1 Corinthians 6:19-20). These words from Paul to the church at Corinth may sound surprising to anyone who is convinced that the New Testament writers were uniformly disparaging of the human body. But this is not an isolated passage. In Romans, Paul urges members of the church "to offer your bodies as living sacrifices, holy and pleasing to God—this is your spiritual act of worship" (Romans 12:1). Clearly, if Paul believed that our bodies were irredeemably corrupted by sin, he would not speak of them as "the temple of the Holy Spirit" or as "living sacrifices" to God.

While it is true that some passages in Scripture seem to suggest that the body and spirit are at odds with each other, an even deeper biblical theme points to their essential unity. Both body and spirit are capable of sin and both body and spirit can be redeemed.

Put negatively, sin is not only a problem of the body. Sin affects the whole person, both flesh and spirit. After all, Adam and Eve's sin was pride, not the lust of the flesh or a physical appetite for apples. One consequence of sin was indeed the reality of physical death. But sin also led to spiritual death. Thus, when Paul uses the term *flesh* to describe the fallen nature of humanity, he almost always is referring to *both* the body and spirit in their rebellion against God. But the opposite is also true: just as the spirit can participate in sin (see Colossian 2:18), the body can also be spiritual (see 1 Corinthians 15:44). Since sin has affected the whole person—both body and spirit—then redemption from sin must also affect body and spirit. This means that the Christian's body as well as the spirit must be saved.

Here we turn to the positive news. According to Scripture, the body is part of creation that God pronounced good. Our bodies are a gift to us, not a curse. God shaped the human form, and when God breathed life into it, our bodies became an integrated union of body and spirit. No person is whole without both. Because our finite bodies bear within themselves the divine image of God, they should be honored, even in their finitude.

The incarnation of Christ is a radical demonstration of the potential goodness of both the body and the spirit. The incarnation is God's stamp of approval on the physical world and a reaffirmation of the claim in Genesis of the essential goodness of creation. Jesus lived a fully embodied life, and because he came to us in human form—not just as a cosmic Savior—our own embodied lives are also blessed as we walk in his steps, like his disciples, growing each day into his image and likeness. "To this you were called," we read in 1 Peter, "because Christ suffered for you, leaving you an example, that you should follow in his steps" (2:21). "Whoever claims to live in him must walk as Jesus did" (1 John 2:6). We do this with our bodies.

How do practices of worship shape us in ways that testify to the living presence of God in our bodies? On the one hand, the question might seem strange since everything we do obviously involves our bodies. But in light of the cultural confusion surrounding the body, I want to focus on five specific areas in which Anabaptist-Mennonite worship can find expression in our bodies and bear witness to the incarnation.

1. Singing: integration of body, mind, and spirit. Unless you are a public performer, you probably don't often think of singing as a form of witness to the world. Yet even if we are not fully aware of it, singing is one of the most deeply formative practices of the Christian church.

Singing is an expression of the incarnation, an explicit moment when spirit and body come together. It begins as a physical activity. We often stand to sing. Sometimes we move our bodies, tap our feet, raise or clap our hands. Above all, singing requires us to breathe deeply and to make audible sounds. It calls on us to make ourselves heard, to give voice to our faith. But singing also engages our full being—our minds and emotions as well as our bodies. The words we sing are often explicit confessions of faith, public proclamations of the content of our belief. In expressing these convictions we are participating in theological conversations that give a particular shape to our doctrine.

At the same time singing touches a part of us that goes beyond the notes or words. In the tension and resolution of chords, in the visual image that suddenly evokes a deep memory, in the texture of the harmony that give voice to our fears and hopes, music shapes us.

Throughout the history of the church, music has been a basic marker of group identity. Within a congregation, music is a collective activity that unites the community in a shared voice. "The one who speaks with me is a fellow human being; the one who sings with me is my brother," claims a German proverb. At the same time, music can also differentiate one group from another—no feature of the Sunday morning worship hour is more likely to evoke praise or criticism than the selection and style of music on a given Sunday!

It is not surprising, then, that music has always played a significant role among groups in the Anabaptist-Mennonite tradition. The earliest Anabaptist hymnbook—dating back to the 1560s and still in use among the Amish today—consisted mainly of martyr ballads. Sung slowly and in unison, the congregation entered into the story of those who suffered for their faith and imaginatively entertained the possibility that they too might be asked to suffer. Since then, Mennonites have sung a wide variety of songs, borrowing heavily from the German pietist tradition, the Reformed Psalter, the gospel songs of the nineteenth century, and contemporary Christian praise music.

Until recently, many North American Mennonite congregations cultivated a tradition of four-part singing, often unaccompanied. For the attentive participant, singing in four-part harmony requires each person to contribute a distinctive voice, so that each member is hearing their own individual voice while also being attentive to the voices of those around. The individual contribution is essential, but always in the service of a larger whole. The harmony of a cappella singing requires a discipline and self-awareness that results in something more than merely the sum of its parts.

In recent years, the Mennonite church has more intentionally welcomed members from many different cultural backgrounds into its fellowship and expanded its repertoire of music to include hymns in other languages with unfamiliar cadences. This too requires a new kind of listening. And with the integration of new voices and new harmonies, the church slowly adopts a new identity.

Singing therefore nurtures us for Christian witness. Though we almost never think about it in this way, singing is practice for living in the world as integrated human beings, fully in tune with our bodies, minds, and emotions. Through singing, a host of Scripture verses, affirmations of faith, words of comfort, and reminders of God's love become deeply embedded in our very being, so that these words and feelings become part of who we are. Christians who frequently worship in song often discover that fragments of a hymn or the lyrics of a chorus will suddenly come to mind, unbidden, at precisely the moment when it is needed most. It is no accident that Anabaptist martyrs often went to their death singing. This was not because they were "happy," in the common meaning of the word, but because they were certain of the Lord's presence. Singing hymns was the best way they knew to express the joy of the Lord.

Finally, the disciplined practice of hearing our own voice as part of the harmony produced by the larger congregation is training for life in the Christian community. Our contribution to the body of Christ is unique and distinctive; our voice needs to be heard. But it becomes a genuine gift to the world only to the extent that it is woven into a larger set of gifts which, together, bear witness to Christ's living presence in the world. This calls for a capacity to contribute your voice with confidence while also being ready to hold back so that other people's gifts might be used; to be self-conscious without being paralyzed; to listen carefully to the collective voice and respond with the necessary personal adjustments in the interests of the balance and harmony of the whole group.

Like all practices, singing is its own reward. Yet it also is training for Christian witness in the world.

2. Foot washing and the holy kiss: a posture of service and non-erotic intimacy. According to John's Gospel, at the Last Supper, Jesus began the meal with a surprising gesture. He poured water into a basin and washed his disciples' feet. Though the practice was a common expression of hospitality in first-century Palestine, Jesus' disciples were surprised and confused, and Peter strongly protested. Yet Jesus explicitly instructed his disciples to continue the practice:

> Do you understand what I have done for you? . . . You call me "Teacher" and "Lord," and rightly so, for that is what I am. Now that I, your Lord and Teacher, have washed your feet, you also should wash one another's feet. I have set you an example that you should do as I have done to you. (John 13:12-15)

Despite Jesus' admonition to "do as I have done to you," most Christian traditions have not understood these words as a command to imitate foot washing literally. Some look on it as a merely a cultural custom of Jesus' time that has no meaningful contemporary parallel. Other Christian groups were, no doubt, embarrassed by the awkward intimacy of the ritual, which requires postures of kneeling and a form of bodily contact at odds with normal personal interaction.

Anabaptist-Mennonite groups, however, have traditionally regarded the practice of foot washing—along with the holy kiss, which frequently accompanied the ritual—as an ordinance of Christ. That is, a teaching crucial to the right ordering of the church. Anabaptist leaders like Pilgram Marpeck and Dirk Philips considered foot washing to be nearly as important as baptism or the Lord's Supper, and Anabaptist hymnals contained several songs written especially for the occasion.

Although the practices of foot washing and the holy kiss are now waning in some Anabaptist-Mennonite groups, there are very good arguments for congregations to keep these worship practices alive. Foot washing is a helpful reminder of the commitments made at baptism. Since we are baptized only once, memories of our baptism can easily recede into the distant fog of the past. The regular practice of foot washing, linked to cleansing properties of water, calls to mind the forgiveness of sins—both our own sins before God and those we have committed against each other. It also is a tangible reminder that we have promised to walk in the path of Jesus and to journey on that path in the company of fellow believers.

Foot washing enacts our commitment to serve each other within the body of Christ. When we wash each other's feet, we are unavoidably thrust into a posture of submission—not in the sense of being under an oppressive power, but the voluntary submission characteristic of a deep and trusting friendship. In washing each other's feet, the categories of race, class, and education that so often divide us in ordinary life suddenly disappear as we express visibly our fundamental equality before Christ. In foot washing, we practice the habit of yielding to each other; we enact with our bodies a desire to regard each other's good as our own good.

In a closely related sense, foot washing testifies to the Christian commitment to a life of service to others. Throughout his ministry, Jesus repeatedly tried to shake the disciples loose from standard assumptions about power. "If you want to be great," he told them, "be a servant" (see Matthew 20:26); if you want to enter the kingdom of heaven "you must become like a child"(see Matthew 18:3); if you want to be first, go to the back of the line. This was not a perverse or masochistic attitude of self-hatred. Instead, Jesus was challenging his disciples to cultivate an attitude of humility, transparency, and vulnerability rooted in the confidence of God's abundant love.

To be sure, the disciples frequently seemed to be tone deaf to his teachings. But at the Last Supper, Jesus tried once more to communicate this foundational teaching of his entire ministry. By washing his disciples' feet, he offered them a physical, embodied demonstration of self-giving love—a love that would ultimately be expressed in his death on the cross. When we repeat that gesture, we take a small step toward being molded into the image and likeness of Christ, which means a life of sacrificial love for the world.

Finally, the physical intimacy of foot washing often concluded in the Anabaptist-Mennonite tradition with the holy kiss, sometimes called the "kiss of peace" or "kiss of love" (see Romans 16:16; 1 Peter 5:14). Both foot washing and the holy kiss are gestures of vulnerability, love and intimacy that are not charged with sexual overtones. In a North American context where the pursed lips of a kiss are almost always regarded as erotic or seductive, foot washing and the kiss of peace are powerful practices that challenge and transcend these cultural assumptions. It is possible to imagine physical forms of intimacy that are not erotic!

Foot washing and the holy kiss are worship practices that shape Christians for a life of joyful mutual submission to each other. In these practices, Christians physically enact the unity of the body of Christ and bear witness thereby to the restoration of humanity to God's intended purposes. At the same time, they remind us that service to others is a measure of true greatness, and that physically intimacy that need not always be charged with erotic overtones.

3. Celebrating God's abundance: fellowship meals. Another way we bear witness to the transforming presence of God in our bodies is by redeeming our relationship with food. As we have seen, modern people tend to have a tortured relationship with food. We love to eat, yet we are often tempted to look on food as merely fuel for the body—something that we "shovel in" or "wolf down" to keep our bodies alive. The promise of "fast food," which regards food preparation as a necessary evil, only reinforces this view.

Asking how we might witness to our cultural confusion about food is an enormously rich topic, extending into such questions as food production, world hunger, physical health, and creation care. Here I want to focus on only one seemingly trivial church practice, one that some might even doubt counts as a worship practice: fellowship meals.

In a fellowship meal—sometimes called a "carry-in" or "potluck"—members of the congregation bring a dish or two to share in a common meal following the service. Mennonites are certainly not the only group to practice this tradition. But fellowship meals have been a long-standing and revered practice that many Mennonites have come to assume as an integral part of the church's life. And with good reason.

A fellowship meal satisfies hunger, of course; and it usually offers the promise of a rich and delectable array of options. But beyond its caloric and culinary delights, fellowship meals as a worship practice can also become an extension of the Lord's Supper—a celebration of God's abundance in which the community is re-formed in body and spirit through the living presence of Christ as it gathers in the simple act of eating. Fellowship meals celebrate God's extravagant generosity: tables are heavily laden with salads and casseroles, ethnic dishes and community staples, vegetables and desserts, in all their colorful and aromatic splendor, set before us like a feast. Here is the tangible, physical evidence that God has blessed and sustained us—a visible sign that our prayers for "daily bread" have been answered a thousand-fold. In its very excess, a fellowship meal invites us into the joy of God's abundance.

It is also significant that fellowship meals are *shared* meals. Each person contributes a particular item of food: each brings a specific and unique gift. But the totality of the whole is always more than the sum of its parts. The meal becomes a feast only as the individual contribution of each member is integrated into the whole. In this sense, fellowship meals reenact the nature of the Christian community itself. In a familiar metaphor, Paul describes the church as a body made up of many different parts, each with its own crucial role to play. "Now you are the body of Christ," he concludes, "and each one of you is a part of it" (1 Corinthians 12:27; see also 12:12-26). Each of us brings particular gifts to the church that are essential to its functioning, yet it is only when these gifts are joined together that the congregation becomes more than its individual parts and is transformed into the living body of Christ.

Fellowship meals are also an occasion for Christian hospitality. Strangers who happen to visit church on that Sunday are warmly welcomed to the table; there is always enough, and more than enough. So the meal becomes not only a celebration of the community in its established identity, but also a sign of a community still in formation—a community whose boundaries are porous enough to welcome newcomers to the feast. In fellowship meals, family units are usually seated in scattered locations so that all people—regardless of age, class, ethnicity, or marital status—join together around a common table, in recognition of the church as our "first family."

Of course, as with every worship practice there is always the possibility of things going wrong. Fellowship meals can be an occasion for gluttony. At times families huddle around their own tables, reinforcing a sense of loneliness for visitors and singles. Potlucks can also become a competitive arena filled with anxious comparisons over who has brought the best dish.

But as a practice of the church, fellowship meals celebrate the abundance of God's creation; they point to a unity that depends on, yet transcends, the gifts of each individual. And they communicate to visitors that the table of God's fellowship could include them as well. Rightly understood, a fellowship meal offers a foretaste of the wedding banquet of the Lamb. It points us toward a time when all God's people will gather from every tribe and nation to sing praises before the throne and then join together in a lavish feast—not merely as fuel to satisfy our bodily hunger but in celebration of God's abundance and the wholeness of all creation (see Revelation 19:6-9).

4. "Let the children come to me": care for the vulnerable among us. "Let the little children come to me," Jesus said, "for the kingdom of God belongs to such as these" (Luke 18:16). Every Sunday morning in our small congregation, shortly before the sermon, someone invites all the children to come to the front of the church for a brief story—told in simple language, usually with visual aids—related to the central theme of the service. Children's time, as we call it, is a worship practice that reveals a great deal about our attitudes toward those in our fellowship who have limited understanding of Christian faith. Unlike some Christian groups that assume children are born sinful, the Anabaptist-Mennonite tradition has taught that children come into this world completely innocent. Created in the image of God, children remain under the tender protection of God's mercy.

More than once, Jesus pointed to children as examples of what it means to be a true disciple. When he wanted to make a point about humility, Jesus called a child to stand in front of him and said, "Unless you become like children you cannot enter the kingdom of heaven. Therefore, whoever humbles himself as this little child is the greatest in the kingdom of heaven, and whoever receives a little child like this in my name receives me" (Matthew 18:3-5). In another context, Jesus said, "Truly I say to you, whoever does not receive the kingdom of God like a child will not enter it at all" (Mark 10:15).

In the regular practice of calling children to the front of the congregation, we are reminded in a tangible way of the radical nature of the kingdom of God. This is a community that turns normal assumptions of human status and influence upside down. What matters most here is not education, theological training, wealth, or family lineage. Rather, followers of Jesus will be known by their trust in God, by their innocence, and by the way that they treat others who are trusting and innocent.

One way we do this is by honoring children each Sunday at children's time. But another way this worship practice finds expression is in the special care that the church extends to other vulnerable members, especially the elderly and those with disabilities. Our cultural focus on minds and bodies that are strong, healthy, and young is driven in part by our deep fear of the dependence and helplessness that we associate with vulnerability. Yet the reality is that every community has members who are born with disabilities, bear lifelong consequences of accidents, or are afflicted with the infirmities of aging. In some ways, the integrity of Christian faithfulness—the measure of an authentic witness to the world—can be gauged by how a community treats those in its midst who are most vulnerable and require special care.

Care for the vulnerable—sometimes understood as an extension of the principle of mutual aid or "bearing one another's burdens"— has been a long-standing practice within the Anabaptist-Mennonite tradition. Many Dutch Mennonite congregations in the seventeenth and eighteenth centuries, for example, founded homes (*hofjes*) specially designed for the needs of the disabled or impoverished elderly in their midst. In addition to creating several well-equipped hospitals, Russian Mennonites in the early twentieth century established a mental hospital, several schools for the deaf and blind, and a variety of mutual aid programs that were the forerunners of modern forms of health insurance. Following World War II, Mennonites in North America took the lead in promoting improvements in mental healthcare in the United States; they were instrumental in the creation of the National Mental Health Foundation and fostering a fundamental transformation in American legal and cultural attitudes toward mental illness.

Today, direct care for the disabled and elderly has been largely outsourced to social service agencies, and costs are borne by insurance companies rather than the church. Yet congregations continue to bear witness to the body of Christ in the hospitality they extend to those with special needs.

It is precisely in our treatment of the vulnerable in our midst that we come face-to-face with the fact that we are more than merely our bodies. To treat bodies that do not meet our cultural standards of beauty with love and respect testifies that God's Spirit is present in every individual, regardless of her or his physical status. Care for those who live with physical or mental disabilities honors the dignity of each person, which cannot be reduced to a set of skills valued by a productive society. The church also honors the vulnerable in its midst with such gestures as:

- ensuring that church buildings are accessible;
- offering respite care for parents of children—and the children of parents—with special needs;
- treating members with mental illness with gentle compassion;
- offering the gift of time and respect to those suffering from dementia, even when the spirit seems vacant or unlovely;
- patiently absorbing some of the manic energy of a person with bipolar disorder.

All of us await with anticipation the full redemption of our body in heaven. But until then we honor the divine image of God in all people when we treat those who are most vulnerable in our midst with dignity and respect.

5. Funerals: dying well as a Christian practice. Between 1974 and 1987, the Mennonite church in Ethiopia lived under a communist military regime extremely hostile to their faith. The government made it illegal to gather for public worship, imprisoned key leaders, and threatened to punish others who openly supported the church. Amazingly, however, it was precisely during this period of persecution that the Meserete Kristos Church experienced rapid growth. One mission strategy in the midst of these difficult years focused on funerals. Since the government still permitted people to gather to bury their dead, the church took advantage of these services to speak openly about their faith, knowing that there would be a wide range of people in attendance.

On the surface, funerals might seem like an odd form of missionary outreach. After all, the Christian faith celebrates life. But in sharp contrast to our cultural anxiety about death, Christians do not reduce life to the physical body, nor do we regard death as a defeat.

Christian funerals are therefore wonderful opportunities to bear witness to the most basic themes of the faith:

- God is the creator and sustainer of life;
- the death of our physical bodies is an outcome of sin;
- in his resurrection, Christ has emerged victorious over the powers of sin and death;
- because of the resurrection, those who die in Christ can anticipate their own resurrection and eternal life with God.

This does not mean that Christians are unaffected by the deaths of those close to them. But it does put death into a larger framework. Christian funerals remind those present that, in the resurrection, God has triumphed over death. Christians, therefore, do not need to fear death or defend their bodies at all costs or desperately cling to life by pursuing every imaginable medical option. With the prophet Hosea and Paul the apostle, they can ask with confidence, "Where, O death, is your victory? Where, O death, is your sting?" (1 Corinthians 15:55; see also Hosea 13:14).

Participating in the funeral services of Christians helps to shape us into the kind of people who know what it means to die well. During the sixteenth century, several thousand Anabaptists were executed for their convictions. Even as these executions increased in number, the movement continued to spread. Indeed, martyrdom became the occasion for a powerful form of witness that attracted many skeptics to join the Anabaptist cause.

Many of the accounts collected in *Martyrs Mirror* highlight the moving sermons preached by the condemned prisoner to the crowd gathered for the execution. They describe in detail the hymns sung, the prayers offered, the letters written, and the words of encouragement given as a final testimony to their faith. Authorities often tried to prevent these opportunities for public witness by cutting out the condemned person's tongue or affixing a tongue-screw to impose silence. But in the end, the stories of faithfulness unto death could not be silenced. The martyr's death offered a more powerful and eloquent testimony to the Anabaptist understanding of the gospel than any sermon they ever preached.

Over time, Anabaptists developed a "theology of martyrdom," which suggested that persecution, torture, suffering, and death were concrete evidence of God's presence in a sinful and fallen world. "Precious in the sight of the LORD is the death of his saints" (Psalm 116:15). The Anabaptist martyrs were seen as continuing a witness that began with Christ, Stephen, the apostles, and the early church. Martyrdom became a seal of God's approval of a Christian life well lived, a crown of glory and life.

Although Mennonites in North America no longer face life-threatening persecution, Christians around the world continue to practice their faith at great risk to their physical well-being. In a culture that fears death and regards preservation of the body as its highest priority, worship practices that prepare Christians to die well offer a powerful witness to the world of the life-affirming truth of the gospel.

Conclusion

Since my short stint on the Appalachian Trail, I have developed a much deeper appreciation for the biblical claim that the goodness of creation includes our bodies. When we read in Genesis that humans are made in God's image, that image includes our physical bodies, and it means all bodies: large and small, fat and skinny, healthy and sick, young and old, fully functioning and partially functioning. God did not make a body and put a soul into it, like a letter into an envelope. Instead, writes Wendell Berry, "He formed humans of dust; then, by breathing His breath into it, He made the dust live. The dust . . . did not embody a soul; it became a soul."[6] Because our bodies are the means by which God is visible in the world, they are precious. Shaped in the image of God and pronounced by God to be good, they are holy—intended by God to be honored, loved and respected.

This view of our bodies has prompted me to rethink the place of our "natural" inclinations and our desires. I am not naive about the human capacity for sin and deception. But I no longer believe that the desires of the body are always enemies of the spirit. Indeed, if we examine our desires more closely, we may discover that even our physical yearnings and passions point us to God. Seen as rightly ordered desires, our hunger for food can lead us to give thanks to an abundant God; our cravings for sleep can point us to the profound wisdom of Sabbath rest; the temptation of lust can yield to a prayer of thanksgiving for beauty; and even the very finitude of our bodies—the fact that I now wear bifocals, that my knees sometimes ache after running, that each morning I am a day closer to death—is an occasion to give thanks for the sheer gift of life.

Perhaps the best news of all is the simple fact that our bodies—our physical, thinking, feeling selves, full of yearnings and hopes and fears and limits—are blessed. In celebrating the blessing of our bodies, we testify to the incarnation, and we participate in God's reconciling presence in the world.

6

Bearing Witness in Our Families

In the fall of 1538, city officials in the Dutch city of Rotterdam arrested Anneken Jans, a young widow who had been overheard singing an Anabaptist hymn. Civil authorities quickly tried Anneken and sentenced her to death by drowning for the threat that she posed to the political and religious order of the city. The etching that accompanies the story of Anneken Jans in the *Martyrs Mirror* captures a particularly painful moment of the drama. Just before her execution, we see Anneken holding out her fifteen-month-old son along with a purse of money to anyone in the crowd who would promise to care for the orphaned little boy. In a letter written immediately prior to her death, Anneken expressed her final wish:

> My son, hear the instructions of your mother; open your ears to hear the words of my mouth. . . . My child, do not regard the great number, nor walk in their ways . . . but where you hear of a poor, simple, cast-off little flock, which is despised and rejected by the world, join them; for where you hear of the cross, there is Christ; from there do not depart.[7]

Modern people may be tempted to dismiss this decision as delusional, self-centered, and irresponsible, especially since authorities gave her the option of recanting. Yet Anneken, steeped in the Gospels, knew that Jesus had repeatedly warned his disciples that following him could mean breaking ties with other allegiances, including those to family. Consider, for example, these stark instructions to his disciples: "If anyone comes to me and does not hate his father and mother, his wife and children, his brother and sister—yes, even his own life—he cannot be my disciple" (Luke 14:26). When one of Jesus' followers wanted to return home to attend the funeral of his father, Jesus retorted, "Let the dead bury their own dead" (Matthew 8:22). A few chapters later, when his mother and brother sent word that they were eagerly waiting to see him, Jesus brushed them off, telling his disciples that they, not his earthly relations, were his true family (see Matthew 12:48-50). We also know that the apostle Paul and several early church fathers regarded marriage as a potential distraction from our love and service to God (see 1 Corinthians 7:9).

To be sure, these are not favorite texts for most pastors. They sound especially harsh to contemporary Christians in the United States who regard "family values" as a crucial measure of the nation's health. Perhaps Jesus was speaking figuratively here. Maybe Paul assumed that the end of time was near. In any case, Jesus *must* have believed in family values!

At the very least, these verses challenge us to look at the family more closely. After all, families are the primary setting in which most of us are nurtured. Here lifelong habits and attitudes are formed; here is where we learn the meaning of love, vulnerability, trust, and intimacy. Yet the family is also a source of much personal anxiety and cultural debate. Because family is such a central, deeply contested institution, this chapter considers how Christians might bear witness to God's presence in their families. How do our worship practices find expression in the daily routines of family life? How might such practices transform our families as a genuine witness to the world of the good news of the gospel?

Biblical Themes: Families As an Expression of the Incarnation

One New Year's Day when I was nine or ten, I decided to read through the New Testament from beginning to end. Eager to plunge in, I started with the first chapter of Matthew and immediately encountered a major problem. The opening lines of the New Testament begin with a long and tedious genealogical list that starts with Abraham and slowly wends its way forward across the centuries until finally arriving at Jesus. Luke's Gospel offers a similar family history, but works backward, beginning with Jesus and going all the way back to Adam and Eve. What a strange thing to include in the Gospels! What could this family record-keeping possibly have to do with the good news of salvation?

The answer, once again, points us to the incarnation. The writers of the New Testament thought it was crucial to remind their readers that Jesus was not just a disembodied Spirit floating down from heaven. To the contrary, they make it clear that Jesus grew up in a *particular* family, in a *particular* culture, at a *particular* moment in history. Like you and me, he had a family tree. He had mannerisms that reminded people of his parents, he had a genetic code that determined the color of his eyes, and he had a lineage and tribe that helped to shape his identity. In short, Jesus had a family.

Like bodies, families, with all their glories and blemishes, are inescapable. Like it or not, you have certain traits that were passed down to you through no choice of your own: a cowlick, a dimple, a pigeon-toed posture, a distinctive earlobe. Some of us are good at things—music, athletics, math—not because we work at them terribly hard, but because they "come naturally." But our family legacy is not just about genetics. We also inherit from our family a language—a particular way of talking and communicating. Family culture instills in us distinctive understandings about what is "normal"—standards of cleanliness or attitudes toward time or our view of strangers or notions about money.

We like to think of ourselves as individuals, yet we can never fully escape our family identity. Among her Amish relatives, my wife is identified not by her professional accomplishments but by an extended family lineage that stretches back at least four generations. Thus in her home community she is known as Andy-Jake's-Mart-Andy's Ruth. For better or for worse, we are tied to our families in ways that go beyond our ability to fully recognize or to change.

For many of us, these family experiences are wonderful. Family means security, comfort, and the solid assurance that we are loved unconditionally. When it feels like the world is falling apart, we know our homes to be places of refuge. In the Old Testament, children were clearly understood to be a sign of God's blessing. Part of God's covenant with Abraham included the promise that his descendants would be "as numerous as the stars in the sky and as the sand on the seashore" (Genesis 22:17). Almost always, flourishing families in Scripture are an indication of God's favor.

Yet any setting in which we are vulnerable and intimate is also likely to be an arena of deep pain as well. Unfortunately, half of all marriages in the United States ultimately end in divorce—divorces that are often preceded by a great deal of anguish and heartache. For far too many people today, family memories are haunted by the reality of domestic violence, emotional trauma, and dark secrets of abuse.

Part of the power of the biblical story is that the families it describes—like our own—are far from perfect. As it turns out, the genealogy of Jesus so carefully recorded in Matthew and Luke is a closet bursting with skeletons. The Savior of the universe came from a very tangled and crooked family tree.

Take, for example, one of the most basic stories in Scripture: the account of Abraham and Sarah. Next to Adam and Eve, this is the original family story in the Bible. Indeed, three of the world's major religions—Judaism, Islam, and Christianity—trace their origins to "Father Abraham." Yet his family life was not very pretty. At one point early in their sojourn, Abraham offered his wife as a concubine in an attempt to appease hostile strangers. Later, when it seems as if Abraham and Sarah would never have a child, they agree that Abraham would sleep with Sarah's maid, Hagar, who gives birth to

Ishmael. Then, when Sarah actually does give birth to a miracle baby, they send Hagar and Ishmael into the desert to die. The family story of their firstborn child, Isaac, is no less messy or tragic. Isaac's sons, Jacob and Esau, hate each other with a white-hot passion, and Isaac's grandchildren sell one of their own siblings, Joseph, into slavery.

Clearly, the family lineage that led to Jesus the Messiah is full of imperfect and flawed people. Indeed, numerous stories in the Bible seem to make a mockery out of the modern notion of family values.

Yet the Bible does not flinch from telling these stories. Just as our bodies have not escaped the brokenness of the world, our families are sites of sin and pain. But they are also settings for the incarnational presence of God, places where the transforming work of Christ can be revealed. In fact, it is often precisely in the places where our lives are most broken or confused that God's grace and healing is most visible.

Families As a Complex Blessing in Anabaptist-Mennonite History

As Anneken Jans's story suggests, sixteenth-century Anabaptists believed that the Christian's allegiance to Christ and the church should take priority over human relationships within the biological family. In practical terms, this meant that one's baptismal vow was not just an individual confession of faith before God but also a public commitment to become part of a new community. The church functioned as a kind of expanded family—the "family of God"—defined not by biological kinship but by the intimacy of relationships shaped by the practices of worship.

Like families, Anabaptist congregations were settings for giving and receiving counsel, for the free exchange of time and possessions, and for nurture and discipline even in matters that most of us today regard as "private." Many of the seventeenth-century *Gemeindeordnungen* (church disciplines) of south-German Mennonite congregations, for example, asked members not to take out loans before consulting the congregation. They assumed responsibility for the care of widows and orphans, and they explicitly addressed issues of sexuality and marriage, even stipulating that Mennonites could marry only "within the church."

So one theme in the Anabaptist-Mennonite tradition is clear: allegiance to Christ and identity with the church redefines the meaning of family—the church is our "first family."

Yet it would be wrong to suggest that the only lesson from the past is that biological families are somehow an obstacle to Christian faithfulness. The same tradition that recounts the story of Anneken Jans has also preserved numerous other stories celebrating the unity and strength of family bonds as a gift from God.

One such story, frequently told in Mennonite children's literature and Sunday-school curricula, sounds like it might have come from the Bible. It begins with a patriarch, like Abraham of the Old Testament, who has left the familiar comforts of home behind. Like the children of Israel, the family embarked on a dangerous journey before settling in a new land, a promised land, where they hoped to start afresh and to reestablish a community that would find favor with God.

In September 1736, Jacob Hostetler left the Palatinate in Germany and immigrated to the "new world" of Pennsylvania. By 1748, he and his wife and children had settled in Berks County, Pennsylvania, where they built a cabin, planted an orchard, and hoped to prosper. But the land he and others had settled had been taken from the Native peoples only a few years earlier. One moonless night in the fall of 1757, Delaware Indians from the region surrounded the Hostetler cabin, intending to do harm. The oldest son, hearing voices, opened the door and was met by a gunshot. He was wounded in the leg. Immediately, the other boys grabbed their hunting rifles from the mantle and took aim at the shadowy figures outside. But just as they were about to pull the trigger, Jakob grabbed the guns and said, "It is not right to take another person's life, even to save your own!"[8]

Oral tradition recounts numerous other fascinating details to the story. After the Indians set fire to the cabin, the Hostetler family, huddled in the basement, saved themselves from burning by dousing the flames with cider they had in storage. When morning came, they assumed that their attackers had left. But just as they were crawling out of the basement window, a young warrior spied them. He raised the alarm, and the Indians returned. Jacob's wife, a daughter, and one of his sons were killed immediately, while he and two of his remaining children—Joseph and Christian—were taken prisoner. As they parted from each other, according to the story, Jacob admonished the boys "not to forget the Lord's Prayer . . . even if you should forget your German language."

Adding to the poignancy and enduring power of the story is the account of their subsequent experience in captivity. The captured Hostetler boys reportedly adapted quickly to their new culture. Joseph was even formally adopted by the Indians. His white blood ceremonially "washed out," he was redressed in Indian clothing and proclaimed by the tribe (in language that sounds suspiciously biblical) to be "flesh of our flesh and bone of our bone." Christian was also apparently adopted by an older Indian man whom he came to love. After the old man's death, Christian chose a younger Indian as his new brother.

But throughout these events, the bonds of the biological family were not forgotten. In a daring move, Jacob escaped his captors and eventually returned to his community. Several years later, Christian suddenly appeared at the home of his Mennonite relatives, dressed as an Indian. Unrecognized, he announced in broken, scarcely recalled German, "Ich bin der Christ" (my name is Christian), whereupon he was tearfully embraced by his family. Joseph, the second son, was finally released by treaty in 1764 or 1765. But only after "long hesitation" did he decide to leave the Indian "customs and manner of living." He maintained a close friendship with the Delaware Indians for the rest of his life.

Contemporary Mennonites retell the story in part because it brings a powerful element of color and drama to their history. But the real appeal of the story likely has to do with its theme of family: the account of several tragic and violent deaths; the ancient theme of family members separated and united again; and, not least, the fact that the story is recorded in a massive Hostetler genealogy of 1912, linking the account to thousands of Jacob Hostetler's lineal descendents.

This is indeed a story about family. But its celebration of the centrality of the family is much more complex than may appear at first glance and is worthy of a closer look.

1. Families as the setting for Christian education. One of the most enduring images of the story is Jacob's insistence that the boys put down their hunting rifles as they attempted to shoot the intruders. In that moment some of the deepest Anabaptist-Mennonite affirmations about Christian pacifism and nonresistant love take on concrete and specific form. Here the story serves as a reminder that allegiance to Christ's way of nonviolent love takes precedence over the natural impulse to defend the family. Yet it is significant that the context for teaching this point comes precisely within the family setting. Some of the most profound lessons of Christian faith in the Anabaptist-Mennonite tradition are not taught or learned in sermons or catechism classes on Sunday morning—important though these settings may be. Rather, Christ's teachings are often passed on in the ordinary decisions, practices, and activities of everyday life that unfold in family settings.

Consider Jacob's parting words to his sons as they were led off into captivity. In the face of impending separation, the question suddenly loomed large: what would be the anchor of their identity? Torn loose from the familiarity of family and culture, how would the boys remember "who they are"? In this anguished moment of truth, Jacob admonished his children to remember the Lord's Prayer, even if they forgot their mother tongue. The source of identity that Jacob hopes they would retain as they move into the unknown was a spiritual, rather than a cultural, legacy. But like the principle of nonresistance, the prayer itself had undoubtedly been imparted to the children as a daily ritual around the family table, engrained in their memories by sheer repetition and a sense of the sacred that it likely had in their home.

2. Family identity is a choice as well as an inheritance. The details regarding the boys' adoption are also relevant to the complex view of family captured by the story. At one level, of course, the story is about the reunification of the Hostetler family, who would go on to propagate a very prolific line of descendents. But even though we know the outcome in advance, the account makes it clear that the boys' return to the Mennonite community and their family of origin was not inevitable. They had, after all, been adopted into new families and new communities—communities that are portrayed as humane and decent despite the atrocities that had been committed against several family members.

When Christian did return, his biological family did not recognize him at first, and he was barely able to remember enough German to communicate with them. Joseph, the story tells us, took years to undo his Indian identity, and he kept some of their customs for the rest of his life. So in the end, Christian's and Joseph's returns to their families required a conscious decision. Of course they had been deeply shaped by the language and perspectives and habits of their family upbringing. But their family identity—like their decision to become part of the family of God—was a genuine choice, a conscious commitment to a tradition and identity shaped by the awareness of other possibilities.

3. Genealogy is not destiny; it is a gift. There is one final theme worth highlighting in this story. As already noted, the fullest account of the story has been preserved in an enormous genealogy of Jacob's descendants that stretches across some two hundred fifty years. Contemporary Mennonites tend to be uncertain about the value of family histories like this. On the one hand, genealogies are probably the fastest-growing Mennonite literary genre. Several internet databases now contain hundreds of thousands of Amish and Mennonite family records, with more appearing every day. Yet hovering around this genealogical activity is a sense of anxiety and even guilt. By its very nature, family history is an exclusive exercise, a clear map of who belongs. In the past, family lineage in many Mennonite circles overlapped with church membership. Today, however, as the Mennonite church becomes more culturally diverse, this preoccupation with pedigree can easily become exclusive and arrogant.

Such critiques need to be taken seriously. But at the same time, Mennonites should be cautious about dismissing this interest in genealogy as mere idolatry or exclusivism. In a culture in which individuals are increasingly isolated and cut off from any connection to the past, a sense of identity rooted in family history can serve as a crucial source of ballast and stability. Moreover, included in every genealogy are the records of new names that have been grafted unto the family tree by marriage or adoption, serving as a reminder that family branches often extend far and wide. These branches, if pursued, will surely link the researcher to still other family names, other traditions, other faiths. The point is not to make the family into an idol, but to celebrate the joy of connectedness—the webs of nurture and care and genuine belonging—that Anabaptist-Mennonites have experienced in their heritage of strong families.

Bearing Witness to the World in the Family

Thus far, I have suggested that the Anabaptist-Mennonite tradition has affirmed the church as its "first family," while also recognizing the biological family as an important training ground for Christian discipleship. If we shift our attention to the present, the question still remains: how might our families—flawed and imperfect though they may be—bear public witness to the incarnation of Jesus? The question is especially pressing in a cultural setting where "family values" has become a lightning rod in a contentious national debate, in which many Christians have been ready to call on the state to defend and promote ideals that appear to be threatened. While these efforts may be well intended, I want to suggest that worship practices, not the state, provide the best foundation for true Christian family values, which are, in turn, a powerful form of public witness to the world.

1. Sharing: bearing each other's burdens. At some point in nearly every Mennonite worship service, participants are given the opportunity to speak openly and spontaneously. The practice of open sharing is sometimes framed as a chance to respond to the sermon, with words of affirmation or an alternative perspective, or even a gentle critique. More typically, however, the time is an occasion for members to express personal concerns. Often framed as requests for prayer, the sharing time allows individuals to communicate details of their life with the larger congregation: news of an illness, the search for a job, a concern for a neighbor, the awareness of suffering in some part of the world. Visitors who are used to worshipping in more formal settings sometimes wince at the level of intimacy in these times for open sharing. Yet behind this worship practice is a desire to draw the body of Christ together in the practices of mutual aid. "Carry each other's burdens," we read in Galatians, "and in this way you will fulfill the law of Christ" (6:2). The burdens we bear—whether they are emotional, financial, or spiritual—are intended to be borne by others in the body of Christ. Sharing time provides practice in doing just this.

During the Christmas break of my second year in college, I was driving to a friend's house one morning when several fire trucks, their sirens screaming, passed me in the opposite direction. I didn't give it a second thought until I arrived at my destination and received an urgent message: "Return home immediately. Your house is on fire!" Long before I arrived, billows of thick, black smoke on the rising about the woods confirmed my worst fears. The house was engulfed in flames. No one was injured, but within the space of an hour virtually all of our family's possessions had disappeared.

Just as quickly, however, our small congregation began to mobilize. First were the countless expressions of condolence. Then, before evening, someone arranged for our family to move into another house. In the week that followed, people from our congregation showed up with food, then clothes, furniture and appliances, and teams of workers to help sift through the debris and assist in the cleanup. In the months afterward, members of our congregation continued the long and patient task of accompanying my family as we relived the grief and set about the hard work of rebuilding a home.

On one hand, there was nothing terribly extraordinary about the community's response; in times of need, people help each other. Yet the reaction was so immediate, so extravagant, so enthusiastic, so genuinely heartfelt as we experienced wave after wave of unconditional generosity. Sharing our joys and sorrows in worship is a practice that prepares us to stand alongside each other during difficult times outside of the worship setting.

A people practiced in sharing their joys and sorrow in worship testify to the good news of the Gospel when they bear each others' burdens in the challenges of life, supporting families in distress and even standing in as a surrogate family when times are difficult.

2. Baptism commitments: fidelity in marriage. At the heart of worship is a relationship with God rooted in a promise of mutual faithfulness or a covenant. Nearly all the Scriptures and hymns in worship celebrate the enduring steadfastness of God's love and mercy. In the Anabaptist-Mennonite tradition, this theme is especially prominent in baptism, in which the congregation welcomes a new member into the community in a joyful service of commitment. Baptismal services almost always include a reference to God's faithful action in history. Just as baptism calls to mind the children of Israel passing through the parted waters of the Red Sea, it also celebrates God's mighty acts and wondrous deeds in the life of the new member, who moves symbolically out of slavery to sin into a new life of commitment and trust. As part of the journey we commit ourselves to a new community whose practices help to form us into the pattern of God's generosity, fidelity, and love.

As a public statement of commitment, rooted in God's loving initiative and the welcoming embrace of the community, baptism also prepares Christians for the practice of marriage. To be sure, the idea of a lifelong commitment to marriage can easily sound naive, especially when we consider how many marriages end in divorce. Indeed, modern culture tends to regard language of *commitment* as a potential burden on individual liberty. If we hold true to our promises, we frequently do so with gritted teeth, under the shadow of legal obligation or because there is a strong self-interest in doing so.

The Christian understanding of commitment, by contrast, begins with an invitation and a free decision. The invitation is to enter into a story of God's persistent faithfulness and love. The decision is to embark on a journey of commitment in the recognition that we are united by the love of Christ, sustained by God's daily gift of grace, and supported by the presence and encouragement of our fellow travelers. To be sure, Christian commitments—whether in baptism or marriage—do have genuine consequences: they narrow the range of infinite possibilities that are part of the modern condition, restricting our freedom and limiting our choices. Not every option is still open to us once we have made a commitment. And yet—paradoxically, miraculously, wonderfully—we discover that those very commitments also give new focus to our choices and open new possibilities for emotional growth and spiritual maturity. "Take my yoke upon you," said Jesus, "for my yoke is easy and my burden is light" (Matthew 11:29-30).

Like our baptismal vows, the vows exchanged at a wedding are never sustained alone; we make and maintain commitments in the context of a larger community that helps to hold us accountable to the promises we have made. Thus some congregations have instituted a formal structure of following up with newlyweds at regular six- or twelve-month intervals during their first crucial years of marriage, or schedule marriage "audits" for all couples on fifth anniversaries. Congregations should be quick to honor couples who have had long and happy marriages and to invite them to share—in all humility—from their wisdom and experience. Anniversary celebrations should happen in churches rather than as private family events.

Just as the journey of faith following baptism can have periods of questioning and doubt, so too marriage commitments can easily go out of focus. This means that the church must be a safe place where couples can share their problems in confidence and trust. We should encourage couples who have been through rocky patches in their marriage to reflect openly on their insights from that experience, thereby making it possible for other couples to acknowledge their own imperfect unions. We need to provide competent counseling with a very strong bias toward preserving marriages. And we should solicit the active involvement of wise people in our congregation to help hold partners in troubled marriages accountable for their commitments to each other and to God.

The point of these specific suggestions is not to make those in our churches who are single, widowed, or divorced feel marginalized.

But in a culture in which fragile and broken commitments are the source of so much pain, the church should bear public witness to the world of the possibility of its members living in healthy, strong, and committed married relationships.

In worship we are reminded of God's unwavering covenant of mercy and love. In Christian baptism and marriage we bear witness to this good news in commitments that are joyful, faithful, and enduring.

3. Extravagant love: child rearing. Some time ago, I saw a movie that has haunted me ever since. *Sophie's Choice*, set in New York City shortly after World War II, focuses on the tangled past of the family of a beautiful Polish woman named Sophie. Sophie survived the Nazi concentration camps. But soon after her rescue from Auschwitz, she tried to take her own life. Slowly, the context of her despair unfolds. During the war, Sophie had become involved in the resistance movement against Hitler. Eventually, she was caught. The Gestapo murdered her husband and sent her and her two young children to Auschwitz.

Not until the end of the movie does Sophie reveal the deep and painful secret of her "choice." On the night she and her children arrived at Auschwitz, a Nazi officer forced her to choose life for one child and death for the other. In a graphic and terrifying scene—worse than any horror movie—she begs them, "Don't make me choose. I can't choose." Her words, of course, fall on deaf ears. When a young soldier is told to take both children away, she releases her daughter, shouting, "Take my little girl!" Sophie can only watch as the screaming little girl is carried away. But her guilt and despair never go away.

The decision at the heart of *Sophie's Choice* triggers a fear deep in each of us: if my mother was faced with that same choice, whom would she choose? At one time or another, all children have wondered just how much their parents love them. We worry that love is finite, that parental affection expressed to one sibling implies a choice not to extend it to another sibling. We assume that there might not be enough love to go around. This is an ancient fear, one of the oldest known to humanity. The Old Testament is filled with stories of siblings doing battle with each other for their parents' affection. None captures these tensions more vividly than the account of Jacob and Esau, twins locked in a titanic struggle over who will inherit the blessing of their father. It is a sordid tale, filled with deceit, hatred, and violence.

But the good news of salvation is that, from God's perspective, the assumptions behind *Sophie's Choice* are just plain wrong. The human impulse is to think of love in terms of scarcity, as if love were finite or needed to be carefully rationed. The good news of the Gospel, celebrated and proclaimed in worship, is that God's love is infinitely abundant. The blessings of love, grace, joy, and mercy that God provides are never limited.

Five years after we were married, my wife and I had our first child. For the next eighteen months we devoted an enormous amount of time and attention to her well-being. At times it seemed that virtually all our waking hours revolved around this single child. As we approached the birth of our second, we wondered whether it would be possible to love another child in the same way. But to our amazement, this was not even a question! Indeed, we went on to have a third and then a fourth child—loving each one just as much as the others. Grounded in the worship of God, Christian families can be settings in which God's extravagant and boundless love finds expression in the way we treat our children. Despite our deepest fears, love is not a limited resource.

The New Testament answer to Jacob and Esau's struggle over who will inherit their father's blessing can be found in Luke 15. Like *Sophie's Choice*, the story of Jacob and Esau is presented as a tragedy. The rules are clear: the blessing must go to either one child or the other. But in the parable of the prodigal son, we discover that the Gospels offer a quite different scenario. Even though the younger son has seized and squandered his inheritance, the blessing of the father is not limited. The gospel is good news because it offers the embrace of God's boundless and unconditional love. There is always enough—and more!

As recipients of God's abundant love, Christian parents testify to the world about the nature of God's love by demonstrating that same kind of love to their children.

4. Bearing witness to the Trinity: porous family boundaries.
Christian worship brings us face-to-face with the mystery of the tri-
une God. Although few of us agonize long and hard over the meaning of the Trinity, we recognize that our language for God does
include God the Father, Jesus Christ, and the Holy Spirit. At the same
time, we also know that the God we worship is one God. Without
exploring all its theological dimensions, at the very least the Trinity
offers the basis for thinking about a kind of identity that is particular
while always in a dynamic relationship that exceeds that particularity.
In the Trinity, a *particular* identity is preserved, but can never be fully
understood apart from the larger whole.

In an important way, Christian families can bear witness to this
wonderful mystery. On the one hand, the particular identity provided
by a family is a profound gift: the gift of a name, a genetic code, a set
of predispositions, a language, and a culture are no small things. Yet
the natural—perhaps even biological—impulse of humans is to
regard these features as firm boundaries within which we barricade
ourselves against the world. This is the assumption, for example,
behind the classic "What would you do if . . . ?" scenario intended to
stump Christian pacifists. The hypothetical intruder in this scenario is
always intent on killing a mother, wife, or child, never a random
stranger who happened to be spending the night. The assumption, of
course, is that defense of our immediate family has a higher claim on
allegiances than almost anything else.

These assumptions are often reinforced by the current cultural
debate about the family. When people talk about preserving "family
values" or promoting healthy families, the image that we usually have
in mind is the so-called nuclear family: a husband, wife, and children
living in a single-family home. But as sociologists and historians like
to remind us, the notion that the nuclear family as an ideal model for
all of society is actually a recent innovation. In fact, throughout most
of human history, including biblical times, most cultures have not
regarded the nuclear family as an ideal. It was more typical for an
extended household of interrelated kin of several generations to live
intermingled with an assortment of servants and hired hands. There

is much to be said for the nuclear family; but to the extent that the ideal family has come to be defined in narrow and exclusive terms and as a refuge of intense privacy, the biblical family may be a source of liberating news.

A Christian view of the family grounded in the Trinity can celebrate the boundaries of family identity as a good thing. At the same time, however, the boundaries of family identity—like the Trinity—are always dynamic and porous. So that even while Christian families celebrate the tight bonds of trust and intimacy, they consciously resist the powerful impulse to privacy and self-absorption and always look for ways that these boundaries can be opened up to others.

Christian families bearing witness to the Trinity might be intergenerational in their composition, ensuring that the elderly are included within the safety and security of the family network. Christian families will be quick to adopt children or to open their homes to foster children—some of the most vulnerable and abused members of our society. Christian families are likely to open their homes to exchange students, to offer temporary housing to people in transition, or simply to provide hospitality to guests who are passing through the area.

Several older couples in my congregation have become, in effect, surrogate grandparents for children in their neighborhoods, absorbing some of the reckless energy of a four-year-old on behalf of a harried parent and providing a bright light of structure, attention, and unconditional love for children whose lives are otherwise filled with lots of uncertainty. Another local couple, moving toward retirement, has decided to rent their basement apartment to single mothers with the idea that they can also serve as friends and mentors, offering a broader perspective and the possibility of stable relationships.

We might even practice our commitment to porous family boundaries by reshuffling our seating arrangements in worship, so that on a given Sunday we would sit as Sunday-school classes or small groups or mentors with those they mentor or even by gender. We would do this, not because we regard family identity as something inherently bad, but as a reminder that family connectedness is not the only relevant category for congregational involvement and identity.

Families bear witness to the Trinity and to the good news of the gospel by celebrating the particularity of identity while also cultivating porous boundaries.

5. Confession: forgiveness and restoration. When Christians gather for worship, they come as ordinary people whose lives are far from perfect. Despite our best intentions, all of us continue to act in ways that go against God's intended purpose for us. This means that gathering to declare anew our allegiance to God in worship must include some time of confession—a public recognition that we have fallen short of the mark.

Sometimes this is understood as a collective confession of our general waywardness, often expressed in a litany or prayer. Other times, there are opportunities in the service for individuals to confess specific sins before the congregation. But regardless of how the confession is framed, worship assumes that a public recognition of our failure is a prelude to forgiveness and to the new freedom that comes with God's renewed mercy and grace. This practice of confession in worship has applications to every area of our life but especially to the setting of family life, where intimacy and the pain of brokenness are so closely mingled.

When I was no more than eight or nine years old, my mom began to reading aloud a book that was very popular among Mennonites at the time. The original edition had been published by Mennonite Publishing House in 1947 and sold more than fifteen thousand copies in hardback before Moody Press began to make a paperback version available to an even wider readership. The odd thing about the book was that by the fourth or fifth chapter, I clearly recall that my siblings and I begged my mom to stop reading; we couldn't bear to hear the story any further.

Christmas Carol Kauffman's *Light from Heaven* tells the story of Annie Armstrong, a Mennonite woman whose husband, Bennet, physically and psychologically abused her and her children. Publicly, Bennet maintained the appearance of a fine, upstanding and honorable man in the church. In the private world of the family, however, he ruled with a kind of reign of terror. Bennet always spent money freely on his own pursuits, while keeping Annie and the children in virtual poverty. At Christmastime he took a sadistic pleasure in wrapping coal and straw in brown paper as gifts for the children. Annie watches in silent horror as he beats four-year-old Joseph, and he continually threatened the family with violence if they would ever speak out.

All along, Annie suffers in silence. "We've tried all our lives to shield Father," she confides at one point to her sister. This shielding of family honor—the fear of public shame—combined with Bennet's regular church attendance, conspire to hide the true anguish and pain that defined the Armstrong family.

To be sure, *Light from Heaven* focused on a rather extreme case of psychological and physical abuse. Readers who grew up, as I did, in a happy and stable home might be tempted to simply dismiss the story as a rare exception. We know that there are problems in other people's families, but we have a mental image of ourselves as people who have strong, healthy, and solid families. Yet Annie Armstrong's story is a painful reminder that church-going families are not immune to the brokenness and alienation.

Because we enter the world as helpless babies, completely unable to fend for ourselves, we are absolutely dependent on others for food, clothing, shelter, and protection. We rely on our families to help us survive in this world—physically, of course, but also emotionally and spiritually. Since the stakes in all this are so high—we are so helpless and vulnerable for so long—children place enormous trust in their parents. Parents are the ones to pull your hand away from the stove, to comfort you when you are sad or frightened or lonely. These same expectations are present in other family relationships as well: spouses depend on each other to be loving, supportive, and faithful; parents want their children to be respectful and kind. Indeed, every member of the family has high expectations for how we want to be treated.

In such a setting, it is almost inevitable that these expectations will be disappointed. In the case of abuse, they will be shattered. Our impulse in the face of these painful realities often is to react as I did as a child encountering *Light from Heaven*: "I don't want to hear about this." So, as in the parable of the good Samaritan, we turn our heads and walk on the other side of the road. Or we turn to our politicians to provide a legal solution to be enforced by law. Or we wax sentimental, hoping that the momentary warmth of a romantic walk in the woods or a diamond ring, lots of chocolate, and a candlelit dinner will "fix" the problems that seem beyond our control. But eventually, many families crack and divide under the strain.

The truth of the matter is that we are deeply flawed people. All of us are extremely adept at self-delusion in our relationships. We hide our flaws; we disguise our weaknesses; we ignore our selfishness; we justify our pride and rationalize our desire for power. All of us could love our spouses or parents more; we could all be less preoccupied with financial security; we could all spend more time with our children or our grandparents. I will never forget the look of astonishment on my daughter's face once when I was working underneath the sink and swore with absolute conviction. Or the time I found another daughter crying in her room when my wife and I had had an argument, and she wondered if we were going to get a divorce. Or the hurt glance of my wife when I broke a confidence in a public setting. None of us are immune from the pain and brokenness of the world, where trust breaks down and fear calls us to retreat into our narrow and defensive worlds.

Christians know that salvation begins by acknowledging our shortcomings; we experience the joy of forgiveness only if we recognize that we have something that needs to be forgiven. So confession is the necessary first step to reconciliation with God and the renewed joy of God's forgiveness and mercy. Confessing our daily dependence on God's love and grace reorients us to the world beyond the self. It cures us of false illusions about ourselves. But at the same time, confessing our shortcomings also reminds us of a standard that has gone temporarily out of focus. So, paradoxically, even as we recognize our failure we are invigorated with new hope and joy and resolve to grow closer to the ideal.

Christian families anchored in the regular practice of confession are uniquely gifted with the possibility of openly acknowledging our shortcomings and admitting our brokenness to God and to each other. Because we have experienced the liberating forgiveness that comes through confession, Christian bear witness to the good news of the gospel when they practice confession and forgiveness within the context of their families.

Conclusion

Acts 8:26-39 records an oddly beautiful story of an encounter along a desolate road between Jerusalem and Gaza. Philip was one of seven people called out by the apostles of the early church to make sure that the needs of the poor were being addressed (see Acts 6:1-7). He was used to ministering to people at the margins. Along the road, Philip happened to meet a stranger described as "an Ethiopian eunuch," who was returning from worshipping at the temple in Jerusalem. By almost every standard, this was a person at the margins. Israel's survival, of course, was based on the family. Throughout Scripture, children are praised as a reward from God, a sign of divine favor. This person was not just a foreigner and a Gentile, but also a eunuch, which meant that he was childless. Moreover, because of his physical condition, he was forbidden by Old Testament law to enter into the temple courts.

When Philip met up with the Ethiopian, the man was reading from Isaiah 53, a passage that speaks about a suffering servant: "He was led like a lamb to the slaughter, and as a sheep before her shearers is silent, so he did not open his mouth. By oppression and judgment he was taken away. Who can speak of his descendents? For he was cut off from the land of the living" (verses 7-8). The Ethiopian's burning question to Philip was, who is the prophet talking about? Is he talking about himself or somebody else?

This passage mattered to the eunuch because he, like the servant in this passage from Isaiah, had been "cut off," without any chance of having descendents. So the question matters to him. Who is this person, he asks, who is "cut-off from the land of the living" without posterity and therefore without future?

That person, Philip replied, was Jesus of Nazareth. He had no family or descendants. Yet *he created the largest family in the world.* He created a new family that knows no boundaries—a home for all who wish to be enveloped in God's love and care. "What is to forbid me from joining his family?" asked the eunuch. "Can I too be adopted, baptized? Look, here's water!"

There was indeed water in the wilderness. There in the desert, Philip baptized the eunuch into the family of God.

7

Bearing Witness in Our Communities

What the gospel needs most is not intellectual brokers or cultural diplomats but rather saints who have taken up the way of the cross and in whose lives the gospel is visible, palpable, and true.

—BRYAN STONE[9]

On July 4, 1585, representatives from the Swiss cities of Zurich, Bern, Basel, and Schaffhausen concluded a series of meetings aimed at eradicating the underground Anabaptist movement, which had persisted in their territories. The mandate they issued was clear: anyone attending an Anabaptist service or supporting their cause would be subject to a series of penalties escalating in severity from fines to banishment to the loss of inheritance rights. In extreme cases, the town governments were ready to confiscate Anabaptist property, imprison them for life, or sentence them into service as a galley slave.

The mandate of 1585 was not new. For nearly sixty years Swiss authorities had been trying to wipe out Anabaptism in their jurisdictions. Throughout the 1580s and 1590s, church and state officials complained that Anabaptists were not only gaining a sympathetic hearing in the countryside but also steadily growing in number. Subsequent mandates followed in 1596, 1601, and 1608, each admonishing local authorities to renewed diligence in their efforts to eradicate the Anabaptists. Three years later, in 1611, the Zurich council issued yet another mandate against the Anabaptists, this time opening the door to the use of physical punishment and even the possibility of the death sentence. A new decree of 1613 echoed this same resolve and likened the stubborn persistence of Anabaptism in the region to a "cancer" that was slowly destroying the body of society itself.

Yet little actually changed. Despite repeated and sustained measures to repress the Anabaptist movement, including the use of spies, fines, forced baptisms, and confiscation of property, religious dissent persisted and even flourish in the countryside surrounding Zurich and Bern.

How are we to account for this phenomenon? Why, in the face of a systematic effort to eliminate all forms of religious dissent, does it appear that Anabaptism continued to find strong support in the countryside?

One window into the appeal of the Anabaptist movement is suggested by the interrogation records of Hans Landis, an elderly lay preacher from the Horgen, just outside of Zurich.[10] Following his first arrest in October 1589, Landis complained vigorously to authorities about the low moral standards and the absence of discipline within the state church. Five years later, at a public disputation organized in the village of Wädenswil, he insisted that the Anabaptists "don't teach anything other than what the Bible instructs and what the apostles did."

Instead of responding to questions about theology, Landis wished to focus on more practical questions of Christian morality. He began by citing the dramatic conversion of a well-known villager who had earlier given himself over to "laziness, gluttony and drunkenness" (*saß, fraß, und soff*) until he encountered the Anabaptists. Once he joined the Anabaptists, the man had changed his life in accordance with the teachings of Scripture, Landis claimed. When one of Landis's Anabaptist friends begged authorities to grant them free reign in the village of Hirzel to see which church would attract more people, Landis argued against the idea, claiming that already "more people are running to us than we would prefer."[11]

An official report from Horgen in 1608 acknowledged the heart of the problem: the Anabaptists, it claimed, were widely known for their moral integrity and their readiness to follow Christ in daily life. Some had even bought property in common and with the income "helped them to support their poor and attracted others to join their group."

References to the Anabaptist reputation for high moral standards as an explanation for their popular appeal became even more numerous during the seventeenth century. In 1644, for example, authorities in Aargau reported that villagers were attracted to the Anabaptists because "they actually followed what was taught [in the Apostles' Creed]."

In December of 1647, Hans Stentz, a recent Anabaptist convert in Kulm, argued in his defense that "the Anabaptists prove the power of the holy gospel through their works, but many among us [Reformed] do not." The court records noted that Stentz "has nothing against our teachings, only the conduct of our life."

A year later Martin Burger explained his defection from the state church because of its toleration of immorality and because "there was no piety in the church. One in front, another behind was always sleeping." When he visited the Anabaptists, however, he discovered "a peaceful and upright people who . . . gladly gave their alms, who loved each other, who refused to swear, who were not immoral despite what [the authorities] said about them." Burger acknowledged that he was not well versed in theology, and he thought most of the Reformed doctrine was good. But "it was bad that the teaching and living did not always agree with each other."

When the local pastor asked the sister of Uli Fischer of Walistolen if it was true that Uli had become an Anabaptist, she testified, "It was just like when the Apostle Paul was illuminated and converted." The Reformed pastor at Lauperswil complained in 1670 that the number joining the Anabaptist fellowship grew every day, to the point where "in some villages they outnumber our own." Even worse, he grumbled, when they were brought before local authorities for disciplining "their testimonies moved some members of the morals court to tears."

These same sentiments found more formal expression in academic circles. Between 1672 and 1693, Reformed theologians in Switzerland published no less than four weighty books against the

Anabaptists, each openly acknowledging the persistent attraction of Anabaptism in the Swiss countryside. In the preface of a lengthy volume written in 1693, for example, Georg Thormann, a Reformed clergyman from Lützelflüh, conceded that "people in the country-side have such a great respect for Anabaptists that many look upon them as holy, as the salt of the earth, as the true chosen people, as the genuine essence of all Christianity. He continued: "It has gone so far that many have the notion that a . . . Christian and an Anabaptist are one and the same thing, and that you could not be a . . . true Christian unless you were or became an Anabaptist." Over the next 610 pages, Thormann sought to disabuse his readers of the notion that the exemplary moral conduct of the Anabaptists was sufficient reason to leave the state church.[12]

Despite more than a century of mandates, threats, fines, imprisonment, torture, confiscation of property, banishments, and even executions, the Anabaptist movement continued to attract new members. Although these newcomers were not always able to articulate a theological rationale for their actions, it was clear that the most compelling appeal of the movement was the evidence of a transformed life.

Mennonites today face none of the legal or physical threats to their existence that their forebears in Switzerland did. Today we are free to share the good news of the gospel whenever and wherever we wish. Missions seminars, motivational speakers, and outreach strategies abound, all offering the promise of church growth. Yet in sharp contrast to Anabaptists in the sixteenth and seventeenth centuries, contemporary Mennonites seem uncertain about what it means to be a truly missions-oriented church.

In the previous chapters I looked at several ways in which worship practices find expression in our bodies and in our families. In this chapter, I want to broaden the scope of witness to ask how our worship spills out into the world in practices that testify to God's presence in our communities and the larger society. I would like to suggest here that an Anabaptist-Mennonite approach to missions assumes that the *content* of the message we are sharing is inseparable from how we *live* the gospel. If this is true, then the practices of worship and witness may be as essential to a truly missional church as our verbal testimony to the good news of the gospel.

Christian Witness in the World: Some Alternative Approaches

One summer several years ago I was traveling by plane to a speaking engagement. I generally enjoy striking up conversations with strangers, and on this day I fell into two back-to-back conversations that have troubled me ever since.

On the first leg of my journey, I found myself seated next to a young couple from Germany. They were keenly interested in politics. When they discovered that I was a Mennonite and a pacifist, they simply assumed that I would line up with them on a whole range of complaints about American foreign policy and the general stupidity of everything that America was doing in the world. I found myself holding back. I do have opinions about various political issues, and I do not support the use of war as a solution to foreign policy disputes. But my commitment to peace is so deeply rooted in my Christian faith and my understanding of God's reconciling work in the world that it's impossible for me to talk about peace without reference to my Christian convictions.

When I began to talk openly of my commitment to Christ, however, the couple quickly became extremely uncomfortable. I could almost hear them thinking, "What a shame! A nice conversation spoiled by someone talking about things that really should be kept private." Somehow sharing personal convictions about political matters was an acceptable topic of public conversation; sharing convictions about faith was not.

We landed in Atlanta and parted company, and I continued on the next leg of my journey. I boarded the plane and, in the delay before our departure, I pulled out my pocket New Testament and began to read. It wasn't long before a person sat in the aisle seat next to me. I noticed him smiling when he saw my Bible. "It's nice to have fellowship with a fellow believer!" he said. I agreed. As we began to make basic introductions, I told him very casually that I taught history at Goshen College, a Mennonite school in Indiana. Suddenly, to my astonishment, everything changed. "You Mennonites are pacifists, right?" he asked. "Our country's at war right now. My son is a Marine. And you guys are a bunch of parasites! It just makes me sick!" Then he got up, went to the bathroom, and returned to another seat.

Those two encounters, coming so close together, left me deeply troubled. Why should it be considered embarrassing or inappropriate to speak about faith in public settings? And why is it that Christians themselves can be so divided over how faith finds expression in the public square?

Behind these questions is a debate as old as the church itself. Virtually all Christians would agree that we should witness to the world as "salt" and "light." All would agree that Christians are to be nonconformed to the culture around us, and that we are called to be "in the world but not of the world" (see Romans 12:2). But what does this actually mean? What form does Christian witness take? Just how should the faith we celebrate in church on Sunday morning be expressed to the wider public during the rest of the week?

The available answers to these questions among Christians in North America today can sometimes seem rather limited. On one hand, many Christians assume that the most effective form of witness should take the traditional form of missions, usually understood as proclaiming the gospel and inviting others to "accept Jesus Christ into their heart as their Lord and personal Savior." Even if it might make my German friends uncomfortable, Christians save the world by starting with individual souls.

On the other hand, many Christians assume that their witness to the world should also find expression in politics and public culture. The argument goes something like this: since the state and the media are the most influential forces for change in the world, Christians should use their collective influence to shape legislative policies, elect the right politicians, set the agenda for public debate, and seek to "Christianize" every aspect of our culture.

These are caricatures, of course, but they do exert a powerful influence on many Mennonite churches today. Whereas Mennonite congregations once tried to separate themselves from the world with practices of nonconformity, these options are especially appealing because they hold out the promise of being "relevant," both to individuals in inviting them to Christ and to the broader culture in calling it to live up to the expectations of the Christian church.

This chapter tries to reframe the question of public witness by proposing an alternative to both of these options. The gospel, I suggest, is indeed personal, in the sense that individuals are transformed by an encounter with the risen Christ. But the primary context of salvation is not in the private world of the individual heart but in the public world of the body of Christ. In a similar way, the gospel is indeed about politics in the sense that it speaks publicly to questions of allegiance, the allocation of resources, and the common good. Christians are not called to be apolitical. But the primary focus of Christian politics—the place where a truly Christian politics is practiced—is not in the nation-state or culture in general, but in the body of Christ.

To be sure, salvation is intended for the whole world. But because worship is the foundation of Christian identity—and because worship is embodied and expressed in the visible life of the church—our witness to the world finds expression primarily in the quality of life together in the Christian community rather than in our role as private individuals or as solitary citizens. We are saved in and through the church. The church, as the body of Christ, is the primary beginning point for Christian witness.

Mission Takes a New Turn: Constantine's Conversion

From the very beginning of the church at Pentecost, Christianity has been a missions-driven movement. The book of Acts and most of the Epistles that follow were written in a missionary context as the church struggled to find its way in the midst of rapid growth. For the next three centuries or so, followers of Jesus faced persecution for their beliefs. Members of the early church were often forced to meet in secret, and many of their strongest leaders were imprisoned or martyred. Yet, as frustrated Roman authorities discovered, the execution of Christians often became an occasion for public witness that resulted in even more converts to the movement.

These circumstances changed decisively early in the fourth century when the Roman emperor, Constantine, converted to Christianity. Almost overnight the state, which had persecuted the Christian church, became its friend and protector. Now that membership in the church included everyone within the boundaries of the Roman empire, the church's approach to missions fundamentally changed. By the sixth century, Christianity had become the only acceptable religion of the empire, and Christian emperors put their armies at the disposal of the bishops to enforce discipline against heretics and to compel infidels (nonbelievers) to join the church.

In 800, Charlemagne became the first "Holy" Roman emperor, symbolizing an explicit marriage of spiritual and political power that characterized European life for the next thousand years. Throughout the Middle Ages, Christian knights regularly marched forth on crusades, ready to reclaim the Holy Land by force and to punish or kill in Christ's name anyone they regarded as an enemy of the church.

This same basic pattern of missions continued in the sixteenth century with the voyages of oversea exploration. Wherever the conquistadores landed in the Americas, they were quick to claim the territory for God as well as for their king. In a very short period, thousands of indigenous people in Central and South America were either baptized or executed as the joint forces of church and state moved to claim the land.

With the rise of democracy and the accompanying principle of religious liberty several centuries later, this coercive approach to missions no longer made sense. But the question of how the church's witness would take public form still needed to be resolved.

One dominant form of Christian thought resolved the question by thinking of missions in two distinct, yet interrelated, levels. Because individuals in modern states were free to choose their own religion, Christians would need to persuade their nonbelieving neighbors to declare their personal allegiance to Christ. Thus, one level of missions focused on personal witness that culminated in an individual confession of faith.

At another level, the Christian witness found expression in the political and cultural arena by encouraging Christians to move into positions of authority in government and culture. Thus, Christians should mobilize as a voting bloc to enact legislation that reflected Christian values. Christians should become politicians, lawyers, and judges; artists, sculptors, and poets; film makers, novelists, and journalists; they should write letters to the editor and make their opinions heard to moviemakers and the entertainment industry—all with the goal of pushing society in general in a direction that is pleasing to God. This approach does not use violence, but it is not hesitant about using political forms of coercion assuming that, even if non-Christians initially resisted the political and culture influence of Christians in the public sphere, they would eventually recognize that Christian values are in everyone's best interests.

As a consequence of this approach to missions, Christians became accustomed to separating the private witness of individuals from the public role of Christians within the state. Thus, as private citizens, Christians testified to their neighbors about God's love and mercy and called on them to love their enemies, refrain from judging, and turn the other cheek. In their roles as public servants, however, Christians could not be expected to live according to such idealistic principles. Indeed, Christians in positions of authority might occasionally have to use coercive, or even lethal, violence to promote the common good. God, it seemed, had two characters and two wills: a "public" God, exemplified most clearly in the Old Testament, who sometimes exercised divine violence to punish evildoers and to defend good people from their enemies, and another "private" God, exemplified by Jesus, who called on believers to forgive their enemies and treat everyone with generous compassion.

The Anabaptist Alternative Approach to Mission: Separated unto God for the World

Anabaptists of the sixteenth century represented a somewhat different approach to missions. Like the Catholic Church of the Middle Ages, they thought of missions as being rooted primarily within the church rather than in the actions of isolated individual believers. But unlike the medieval church, they rejected use of violence to advance the gospel, and they did not think that a territory or state could be "Christian." Like Protestants of more recent times, they assumed that missions included a personal encounter with Jesus. But that encounter was not private; it always implied new forms of relationships within the church. Thus, according to the Anabaptists, there was no salvation apart from life in the body of Christ. It was this body—the church—not the state or the media or culture, that was the primary bearer of the good news.

The Anabaptists also did not distinguish between the private morality of the individual Christian and the public morality of a civil servant representing the state. The body of Christ, they insisted, is a public and visible reality, not a private retreat that defers real authority to the state. Since God is most visible to the world in the church, the primary focus of social transformation should find expression for the Christian in the body of Christ rather than the state.

For people used to thinking of the state as the primary center of power, the Anabaptist refusal to participate in the police force or military—combined with their hesitance to run for public offices, serve on juries, or identify with the symbols of nationalism—have sparked confusion and suspicion among other Christians. The Anabaptist intention, however, was never to challenge the existence of the state. Since their primary loyalty was to a defenseless Christ and to the church that shed no blood, they simply regarded traditional forms of politics as inappropriate for extending the gospel.

So, what form does this witness take in the world? How do the practices of worship shape the church so that it becomes a visible testimony to the world around, inviting others to join in God's abundant love and reconciling work? This happens in numerous ways, but here are five specific practices in which worship and witness testify in the public life of our communities to the good news of the gospel.

1. Honoring the Sabbath: beyond production and consumption. "Remember the Sabbath day by keeping it holy" (Exodus 20:8). These words from the fourth commandment given to Moses at Mount Sinai are succinct and clear. For six days God labored to create the world and all that is in it. But on the seventh day, according to Genesis, God stepped back and rested from the good work of creation. So, too, God's people were to enjoy the good work of productive labor, followed by a day in which they set aside their ordinary work to worship God.

The commandment seems simple enough. Yet Jewish tradition—and Christians who share in that tradition—have often struggled to define just what it means to "keep the Sabbath holy." Over time, Judaism developed a complex set of rules that attempted to define the precise nature of those activities permitted on the Sabbath and those to be avoided.

Jesus challenged those defending these laws to reconsider the deeper intention behind the commandment to keep the Sabbath holy. Although he assured the Jewish leaders of his day that he was not mocking Sabbath laws (see Matthew 12), he consistently got into trouble for seeming to ignore Sabbath rules. For example, he did not hesitate to heal on the Sabbath, and he openly defied Sabbath regulations by pausing to eat grain from an open field with his disciples. When Pharisees protested, Jesus responded that the Sabbath was created for humans, not the other way around (see Mark 2:27). God intended the Sabbath as a gift, not as a burden or a threat.

The early church further broke with Jewish tradition by designating Sunday rather than Saturday as the day set aside for Christian worship. Since Jesus rose from the dead on the first day of the week, Sunday became the occasion for Christians to celebrate the resurrection. By the fourth century, Sunday had become established throughout the Roman Empire as the Christian day of worship.

Initially, the Anabaptists do not seem to have elevated any particular day of the week above another for their worship. They gathered for prayer and Bible study throughout the week, and some even went out of their way to work on Sunday as a public expression of their opposition to the Catholic mass. By the end of the sixteenth century, however, most Anabaptist groups had settled into a pattern of Sunday worship. Traditionally, Mennonites groups in North America took God's example of Sabbath rest quite literally. Although practices varied widely, many Mennonite communities prohibited their members from all forms of buying and selling, from participation in sports, and from most forms of entertainment on Sunday.

Although it is easy to dismiss those restrictions today as being legalistic or petty, the practice of honoring the Sabbath offers a witness to the world in at least two distinct ways. First, Christians bear witness to the world by the simple physical act of gathering together. When Christians decide to get out of bed on Sunday morning and join together with other brothers and sisters in the church, they are reenacting the ancient biblical story of God calling out a people for a special purpose. We who were scattered physically are now coming together as the people of God. So we honor the Sabbath, and we bear witness to the world, in the simple practice of coming to church, where we will shake hands, greet people, inquire about each other's health, and eventually move together into a shared experience of worship.

A second way Sabbath practices bear witness to the world is by challenging the impulse in our culture to define our identity in terms of production or consumption. When I was growing up, I chaffed at the restrictions that my parents imposed on what we could or could not do on Sunday. It was quite clear that we were not to do ordinary work around the house on Sunday—certainly not for pay—and wherever possible we also avoided buying anything on the Sabbath. At the time, those restrictions seemed irrational and legalistic. But I have come to a much deeper appreciation for the witness such restrictions may hold for those who honor them self-consciously and intentionally.

The pressures in our society to define human identity in terms of production and consumption are enormous. Our jobs can easily absorb our every waking hour. North Americans today are under

tremendous pressure to work longer hours and to be ever more productive. In a similar way, the pressure in our culture to buy more
things is pervasive. Without really intending to, we can easily fall into
a pattern of working in order to have sufficient money to go shopping
during those few waking hours when we are not working. Sunday,
especially, becomes a day for "recreational shopping," that is, going to
the mall simply to browse and see what new things are available.

By honoring Sabbath restrictions against buying and selling,
Christians offer a visible witness to the world that our identity does
not ultimately reside in the things we make or the things we buy. Our
status and our identity is grounded not in our jobs or possessions but
in the fact that we are children of God, made in the divine image and
created to live in loving and trusting relationships with each other.

2. Scripture: remembering who we are. One basic thing that all
Christians do when they gather for worship is read Scripture. How this
actually happens can vary widely. Sometimes Scripture is read by the
whole congregation, sometimes by a single reader, sometimes as a
responsive reading. At other times it is acted out as a drama or recited
by memory. Some congregations use a common lectionary as the
source of scriptural texts. Some have the congregation stand to hear
the Scripture. Some kiss the Bible before or after reading. But at some
point in the worship hour, every Christian congregation is almost certain to read Scripture.

As a worship practice, the Scripture passage usually sets the context for the sermon. But at a deeper level, reading Scripture every
Sunday is a crucial way of reminding the gathered community of its
most fundamental identity. As we listen again and again to the stories
of God's work in history, we slowly begin to recognize our own place
within the deep flow of that story. And in so doing we discover an
identity—rooted in memory—that gives meaning to our choices and
order to our lives.

A living faith is rooted in the biblical story. In times of uncertainty the children of Israel repeatedly recalled the works God did
with "a mighty hand and an outstretched arm" (Deuteronomy 5:15)
as a way of getting their bearings again. Jesus recognized that the

identity of his disciples was served best, not by giving them lots of instructions or a lengthy list of rules, but by telling stories. When the Sanhedrin demanded that Stephen give an account of his faith, he did not cite a list of doctrines; rather, he began by telling stories of God's wonders and miraculous signs in history (see Acts 7). Memory is the fabric of a community. It is the glue that binds a community together in a shared past and a common future.

My wife's Aunt Nora, an Amish woman, loved to tell stories. The mother of sixteen, Nora was a matriarch in the very best sense: she knew not only the names but also the birthdays of more than one hundred of her grandchildren and great-grandchildren. When we visited Nora, we often gathered around the kerosene lamps in her living room to settle in, along with several of her adult children and a dozen grandchildren, to hear her tell stories. Part of the pleasure of hearing these stories was Nora's rich memory of details and her colorful manner of speech. But it occurred to me once when I was listening to a story that I had heard her tell many times before—it might have been the runaway buggy headed toward an oncoming train or the lantern in the barn or the gruesome details of a logging accident—that the point of the story was not about originality or some new exciting, fresh detail. We were not being "entertained" in the modern sense of expecting to hear something new. Indeed, all of us knew the outcome of virtually every story in her repertoire. The real point of our gathering to hear Nora tell these stories was to be reminded again—precisely by the familiarity of those tales—that we somehow belonged to this circle, that these were *our* stories.

Something similar happens when we listen to the words of Scripture in worship. Because we are a forgetful people, we tell the familiar stories of the Bible and are reminded of our identity as a people of God. Cultivating memory enables us to live in the world with confidence, empowered to speak truthfully about the world, to name the principalities and powers, and to invite the world to align itself around the truth of the Christian story.

3. Offering: sharing our resources. Another worship practice—so common that we scarcely take note of it—is the ritual of collecting money for the larger work of the church. Jesus recognized that the motivations for giving money could be problematic, and he encouraged his followers not to make a great show of their contributions (see Matthew 6:1-4). But the regular collective gesture of offering a portion of our paycheck for the work of the church is a crucial practice of worship that helps to form us for living lives that testify to God's presence in the world.

The practice of offering our resources as a form of worship is not new. In the Old Testament, the children of Israel publicly demonstrated their dependence on God by bringing the "firstfruits" of their harvest or their finest sheep or bull to the temple. It was not that God needed newly harvested grain or a fine young bull to satisfy an appetite. In fact, everything already belongs to God. The gathering of an offering is a symbolic gesture of precisely that fact: by the regular practice of relinquishing our "possessions," we are reminded of the fundamental truth that everything ultimately comes from the abundance of God. Indeed, sacrifices to God in the Old Testament were often burned! What we give to God is ultimately not about redistributing our income but about saving ourselves from the illusion of self-sufficiency.

The New Testament is filled with teachings on the dangerous gift of wealth. On the one hand, money is a reflection of human creativity joined with the fecundity of the earth. Wealth is a tangible sign of excess resources—visible evidence of God's abundance—for which we ought to give God praise. But Scripture warns about the potential dangers of possessions much more frequently than it does about the dangers of violence or sexual license. In our context, of course, amassing a large retirement account and investing wisely in stocks are often considered virtues. Passing an offering plate on Sunday morning is quite distant from offering a burnt sacrifice to the Lord. But the regular practice of relinquishing our wealth is a small, tangible reminder of our dependence on God.

In the Anabaptist-Mennonite tradition this discipline of "letting go" has found concrete expression in the form of mutual aid programs. Thus, Mennonite Disaster Service provides a structure for mobilizing financial and volunteer resources to respond to natural catastrophes. Mennonite Economic Development Association enables business people to share resources and expertise in ways that enable people to provide their children with food and clothing, to earn a decent living, and to enjoy a greater measure of economic security. Mennonite Central Committee assists people around the world who are hungry and homeless.

But the deepest witness to the world is not in the amount of money contributed to good causes. After all, even people who care nothing about worship can do this. Rather, Christians who are formed by the habit of giving testify to the abundance and grace of God by practicing reckless generosity, exuberant giving, and joyful redistribution of their material possessions. As we dispossess ourselves of things, we create a new space to be possessed by the loving care of God.

4. Prayer: patience as a political witness. Like Scripture reading and the offering, the practice of prayer in worship can easily become so routine that we don't give it much thought. When we do start to think carefully about prayer, it sometimes raises questions that seem best left untouched. Petitionary prayers at church, for example, in which we ask God to respond to specific requests, can easily turn God into a cosmic gift dispenser. Do we really think that praying hard will change God's mind about something?

In a similar way, prayers that have been written out ahead of the service can sometimes sound stilted or inauthentic, yet spontaneous prayers can also be fraught with challenges as we try to find appropriate words to capture a multitude of needs or emotions. Outside church, the complexities related to prayer are even more pronounced. In a society of agnostics, atheists, and people of many different religions, Christian prayers at public events often seem like an imposition of one person's faith on everyone else.

Without detracting from the importance of these questions, I would suggest that in the regular practice of prayer the specific content of our petitions may be less significant than the posture prayer cultivates. Ultimately, prayer is an acknowledgment of God's sovereignty and power. Prayer reminds us that God, not us, is in control of history. Prayer cultivates an attitude of vulnerability. It is an exercise in yielding to the will of God recognizing that we are dependent on God for everything—daily bread, health, life itself, including the gift of God's of love, mercy and forgiveness.

Sometimes, the quick response of "I'll be praying for you" becomes an excuse to avoid the messy complication of offering tangible help to the person in need. But so much of modern culture is focused on strategies for "fixing" problems, especially in the public world of politics, technology, and medicine. Modern people assume that the future is in their control, if they only plan, analyze, calculate and legislate carefully enough. In this context, prayer becomes a form of public witness when it cultivates in Christians a capacity for patience, humility and hope. The patience associated with prayer should not be confused with passivity or indifference. Instead, it bears witness to the power of God to work in the world in ways that go beyond our careful plans.

Recently, while visiting friends in the German city of Berlin, I was invited to preach on the theme of Christian peacemaking in a small Baptist church at the edge of the city. As I shared my thoughts on the good news of peace, I was startled by the sight of an elderly man seated near the front who had begun to cry. For the duration of the sermon, tears continued to stream down his face. Afterward, he came directly to me and shared his story. During the Cold War the church had been located in East Germany, in the shadow of the Berlin Wall. For most of the man's adult life, the wall had seemed as immutable as the Swiss Alps—a looming symbol of political tensions and the threat of war. The wall had divided families from each other and made it impossible for fellow believers to worship together. Every Sunday for twenty years, he and a group of friends had gathered outside his church to light candles and to pray that the wall might someday come down.

"People often made fun of us when we gathered here for prayer," the man said. Then, when the soldiers moved in with tanks and machine guns, "all we had were our candles held with trembling hands." But when it seemed like there was no hope, he said—his voice choked with sobs—"the wall came down! The wall came down."

In a world driven by impulsive inclination to action, prayer is a conscious gesture of stepping back to wait, watch, listen, and hope that our desires and our actions will be aligned with God.

In a public context where politicians are prone to speak loudly and act quickly rather than to wait patiently, prayer is a discipline that calls Christians to refrain from jumping into every crisis and to resist despair when it seems that things are going badly.

5. Preaching: the power of verbal witness. In most Protestant traditions, a well-planned Sunday morning service means that all the components of worship—the songs, Scripture reading, prayers—are designed with a view to the main event: a twenty- to forty-five-minute sermon by the pastor. If it were true that Christians simply did what the Bible says, there would be no need for sermons. We would just read Scripture and then live accordingly. Sermons provide a bridge between the text of Scripture and the context of daily life. Precisely because it is an interpretation of Scripture—arguing for a particular reading of the text—many Protestants regard the sermon as the most important part of worship.

The Anabaptist-Mennonite tradition, by contrast, has been somewhat ambivalent about the sermon. On the one hand, Mennonites have tended to be suspicious of "much talk" or "empty words." The authority of the congregation is evident more clearly in the daily life and practices of its members than in the carefully chosen words of a single leader. Some contemporary Mennonites like to cite the words of St. Francis: "Preach the gospel; if necessary use words."

Mennonite skepticism about a sermon-focused worship also reflects an older practice of "the priesthood of all believers." Traditionally, many Mennonite congregations selected ministers from within their own communities as unsalaried, largely uneducated lay leaders and identified them as "teachers" (*Lehrer*) or "leaders" (*Vorsteher*) rather than "preachers" (*Prediger*). The Bible is best interpreted by the collective discernment of the whole congregation rather than the opinions of a solitary preacher. Thus many Mennonite congregations have structured opportunities for members to respond to the sermon either in the worship itself or during the Sunday school hour that follows.

The idea that Christian faith is better demonstrated than taught, better lived than argued, has much to recommend it. Indeed, the central theme of this book has been a defense of the integrity of Christian practices as the primary form of witness. That said, however, the reluctance of many Mennonites to reduce faith to verbal propositions has frequently rendered them nearly mute when it comes to sharing the good news of the gospel with their neighbors.

The reluctance of many contemporary Mennonites to speak openly and enthusiastically about faith is sharply out of step with the early history of the Anabaptist movement. Since Anabaptist leaders had very limited access to pulpits and printing presses, the rapid spread of the movement was due almost exclusively to oral communication and face-to-face contacts. These contacts focused initially on family networks, friendship groups, and occupational circles. An itinerant preacher might go to the home of someone sympathetic to the Anabaptists, read and expound on Scripture to the friends and relatives of the household, and baptize those who were ready to commit themselves to the movement. Rarely were these meetings larger than fifteen or twenty persons.

Historian Arnold Snyder has given a graphic description of one such missioner, a needle seller named Hans Nadler. As he traveled from city to city, Nadler would strike up conversations with people and, according to the court testimony, "whenever he met good-hearted persons in inns or on the street . . . he would give instruction from the Word of God." If a listener was open to hearing about suffering and persecution, and was ready to "abstain from the joys of the world," Nadler would outline how the hearer could "receive the Word of God like a child and . . . be born anew."

Remarkably, Nadler was illiterate. But he developed a system of preaching and instruction based on line-by-line expositions of the Lord's Prayer and the Apostles' Creed, which could be understood by virtually everyone, educated and uneducated alike. Nadler is not noted today as a fiery evangelist or someone who baptized hundreds of people. But his simple, direct approach to missions—somewhat akin to what we today might call friendship evangelism—was typical of Anabaptist missions.[13]

As a practice of worship, sermons consistently put our understandings of faith into words. They offer a dynamic link between the truths of Scripture and the particular context of the listeners. As we listen to sermons, we should not only be attentive to the content, but we might also ask ourselves how these reflection on the Christian faith might be translated into a vocabulary that could be heard and understood by an unchurched co-worker or neighbor.

Despite all of the obvious strengths of a lived faith, we should never discount or disparage verbal testimony as a form of witness. Scripture calls every Christian to be ready to share his or her faith: "Always be prepared to give an answer to everyone who asks you to give the reason for the hope that you have. But do this with gentleness and respect" (1 Peter 3:15).

Christians bear witness to the Gospel when they share the good news verbally with their co-workers, friends and neighbors.

Conclusion

The church and the world have a common Lord. There is one God who has created the universe, who sustains life, who is lord over all. At the same time, the church is "called out" of the world to the extent that it openly recognizes the lordship of Christ. The difference between the church and the world is marked not by the church's perfection but by its public confession—a confession of sin, but also a confession of faith in the One who offers healing from the brokenness brought about by sin. Thus, the primary gift of the Christian witness to the world is an invitation to confession and transformation.

Well-meaning mission-minded Mennonite from both the "peace and justice" and the "evangelical" persuasions face a powerful temptation to be relevant to the world according to the world's criteria. But inevitably, the world the logic of effectiveness or efficiency confuses means and ends, and ultimately leads to coercive strategies justified by the fact that the outcome seems to be righteous.

A witness to the gospel of Christ, by contrast, is vulnerable and cruciform. It resists all violence, even in defending itself. Its driving force is love rather than justice; it invites rather than compels; it trains martyrs, not warriors.

With that in mind, I have suggested in this chapter that the most powerful form of evangelism may be found in the practices of the church, beginning with practices of worship that shape Christians into a community characterized by habits of love, compassion, healing and generosity. Through the quality of its life together, the Christian community helps the world to recognize its own alienation from God, and it invites the world to repentance and transformation.

The holiness of the church is always *for* the world—it is an invitation to the world. In practices of worship and witness the church become a parable for the world, inviting those who have not embraced the path of Christ to imagine the possibility of an alternative way of live grounded in God's love.

8

Bearing Witness in Our Places and Spaces of Worship

About thirty miles southeast of Zurich, in a remote mountainous pass above Lake Zurich, a narrow footpath leads to a natural opening in the rocky facade of a cliff. Accessible only by an arduous hike along a ravine, this wide opening into the mouth of a cave once provided shelter for generations of goat herders seeking refuge from winter blizzards or sudden summer storms. In the sixteenth century, the cave also served as a secret meeting place for Anabaptists hiding from authorities. Their voices muted by the sound of a waterfall tumbling past the face of the opening, worshippers regularly gathered in the rustic opening for singing, Bible study, and prayer.

Today, the so-called Anabaptist Cave (*Täuferhöhle*) is a favorite destination of latter-day Anabaptists, especially Mennonite tourists from North America, who frequently hike to the rocky opening to sing, share communion, and reflect on the faith and commitment of their forebears. I have been there often with families, student groups, and elderly pilgrims, and the effect is always the same: a deep sense of awe and appreciation, and an awareness of God's presence in this craggy, rough-hewn place of worship.

Undoubtedly, the early Anabaptists would have preferred to meet for worship in a more comfortable location. But because they were considered heretics and rabble-rousers, they frequently were forced to gather in hidden, out-of-the-way places. Eventually, Anabaptist preachers made a virtue out of the inconvenience, denouncing the grand Gothic cathedrals of their day as "piles of stone" (*Steinhaufen*) or "houses of idolatry" (*Götzenhäuser*). Christ was present, they insisted, wherever two or three were gathered in his name (see Matthew 18:20). Or they turned to another favorite verse: "the earth is the Lord's" (Psalm 24:1). Since there was no place on earth that did not belong to God, believers could be assured that wherever they gathered for worship—in the kitchen of a home, a watermill, a forest clearing, a lean-to, a prison cell, or even a rowboat in the middle of a lake—God would be in their midst.

The need to meet in secret, combined with these theological convictions, left later Anabaptists and Mennonites deeply ambivalent about the physical spaces where believers gather for worship. The Anabaptist rejection of the notion that certain buildings or images are "holy" encouraged later Mennonites to downplay the significance of church architecture or aesthetics. "What is this place where we are meeting?" begins a favorite hymn of North American Mennonites. The answer is resoundingly functional: "Only a house, the earth its floor, walls and a roof sheltering people, windows for light, an open door."[14]

Today, most Mennonites would be hard pressed to offer a theological rationale for a *distinctly* Mennonite worship space. Mennonites in North America today worship in homes, storefronts, school auditoriums, meetinghouses, church buildings inherited from other denominations, as well as in modern structures that reflect the latest in architectural fashion. The true church, we are inclined to argue, is not the building but the gathered community. The Lord is not interested in elaborate ceremonies; instead, we are "to act justly and to love mercy and to walk humbly with your God" (Micah 6:8).

At the same time, however, to call a worship space "only a house" does not quite ring true. Despite our language to the contrary, the space where we gather is never neutral. Worship spaces are never "merely" functional. As with the incarnation itself, the Spirit is at work in our physical surroundings, often in ways we scarcely perceive.

For many years, my office was situated in the basement of the college library. Although it was somewhat inconvenient for students, I found that it served my basic needs quite well. It was a quiet place to work, I had sufficient space for my files, and I could easily find the books I needed in the library stacks directly above me. Several years ago, however, a library expansion project forced me to relocate my office to the third floor of another building.

To my great surprise, the nature of my daily activities changed almost immediately. Even though my office still served the same basics functions, I suddenly found myself in much closer proximity to colleagues from several other departments. We began to have a brief, daily tea break at which our conversations ranged from teaching strategies to research projects to the joys and frustrations of everyday life. Students visited my office much more frequently as they passed by on the way to classes. And, for the first time, I had a window with natural sunlight and a treetop view of the changing seasons. In some ways, the work that happened in my office did not change. But at a deeper level, the new location gave me a fundamentally different perspective on the context and meaning of my work.

Something similar happens in worship. Even when we are not fully aware of the fact, the spaces in which we gather for worship both express and shape our deepest beliefs. Whether it be a medieval Gothic cathedral, a storefront in a rundown neighborhood, a white clapboard meetinghouse at the corner of a cornfield, a suburban living room, or a megachurch just off the bypass, the physical context of worship affects our encounter with God.

Another reason Mennonites should be cautious about referring to their worship spaces as "only a house" is that our actions do not really reflect the sentiment expressed in the hymn. During the course of the twentieth century, as Mennonites in North America increasingly entered into the cultural mainstream of society, our church buildings slowly began to mirror our new economic and social status.

Today, construction projects on Mennonite churches—be it a renovation or a new building—frequently cost hundreds of thousands, if not millions, of dollars and require complex design decisions involving building committees, architects, interior designers, and contractors. Often these construction projects are a sign of numerical growth and occasions for great celebration. But just as frequently, they bring in their wake fierce internal debates over finances, space priorities, aesthetic judgments, and decision-making authority. Clearly, judged by our budgets and the energy invested in construction projects, our spaces of worship *matter* to us!

Finally, Mennonites should be attentive to the physical spaces of worship simply because of the incarnation. The Anabaptists were rightly suspicious about the human tendency toward idolatry, that is, the human urge to confuse created things with the Creator. Indeed, some Anabaptists were even involved in rampages aimed at defacing or destroying the altars, statues, and stained-glass windows in Catholic churches in order to "purify" them. But the antidote to idolatry is never a wholesale rejection of the material world. Although God can never be *confined* to a specific place or worship practice, as we have seen throughout this book God is consistently made known to humans through the material world. Precisely because God created the earth, was made known in the history of Israel, and was revealed most fully in the human form of Jesus, Christians need to be attentive to God's presence in the medium of the physical world, including the spaces that we set aside for worship.

All this suggests that the buildings in which we worship are more than "only a house." Physical settings have an enormous impact on how we experience worship. Our investments of time, money, and creative energy reflect theological decisions about our worship spaces. Places and spaces matter! Yet in the absence of a positive theological tradition regarding the aesthetics of worship, when it comes to designing their worship spaces Mennonites are likely to fall back into the hodge-podge of individual taste or simply the default mode of whatever happens to be fashionable in the local religious community.

This chapter will look briefly at places of worship in the Bible and then at some developments in the history of the Christian church. Arguing for a distinctive Anabaptist-Mennonite architectural style may be premature. However, I do want to suggest a simple framework for our ongoing conversation—focusing especially on themes of *theology, aesthetics*, and *function*—that is shaped by the insights of the Anabaptist-Mennonite tradition.

Woven into these reflections is a deep appreciation for the wonderful mystery of God's presence in material form and, with that, the awareness that our spaces of worship are a form of visible witness to the world.

Biblical Themes

The temptation among some Mennonites to dismiss our church buildings as "only a house" reflects a lively tension running throughout Scripture over how God and humans connect with each other. According to the biblical story of Genesis, God desires to live in a direct, intimate, face-to-face relationship with human beings. In the Genesis account, God spoke directly with Adam (2:16); God enlisted Adam's help in the naming of the animals (2:19); God came to walk with Adam and Eve "in the cool of the day" (3:8). But as a consequence of the fall, Adam and Eve were ashamed to face God directly. Ever since then, human interaction with God has been through intermediaries of one form or another.

Thus throughout the biblical story, God continually reaches out to humanity through material forms. Consider, for example, the story of the Exodus, which begins with God's appearance to Moses in the form of a burning bush and moves forward amid other spectacular revelations in a series of plagues, the waters parting in the Red Sea, a spring gushing forth from rock, a pillar of fire at night, and manna from heaven. On Mount Sinai, Moses received the Ten Commandments on stone tablets inscribed in solid rock by God's very hand.

Likewise, the human response to God's initiative is expressed in material form. Already in Genesis we see Abel and Cain bringing gifts to God, offering a portion of their labors as a sacrifice of thanksgiving. Throughout the Old Testament this pattern of offering sacrifices serves as a concrete demonstration that everything in creation ultimately belongs to God—that the fruits of the earth come to humans as a gift from God, not as possessions that can be claimed or grasped, and that these fruits are appropriately offered back to God in expressions of gratitude.

At several key moments in their history, the children of Israel built stone piles or monuments as physical reminders of specific instances when God intervened on their behalf (see Genesis 31:44-54; Joshua 4:1-9). The point of these stone piles was not to commemorate the rule of an earthly king or to celebrate a feat of human engineering, like the pyramids of Egypt or the ziggurats of Mesopotamia. Indeed, the prophets repeatedly warn against idol worship or anything that reduces God into a form that can be controlled or manipulated by human beings. Rather, rock piles were tangible markers of God's intervention in human history on behalf of God's people. Encountering them prompted memories of God's saving actions and evoked a posture of thanksgiving and praise.

The physical places of worship took on a new form when the children of Israel settled in the Promised Land. The stone tablets of the Law had been housed in the ark of the covenant, a portable structure that held sacred powers. But as these former refugees became wealthy, King David wanted to build a more prominent and permanent house of worship. Initially, God rejected David's offer to build a temple (see 2 Samuel 7). God was not to be confined to a physical place. However, when David's son, Solomon, persisted, God made it clear that the temple should be built according to very explicit and precise instructions. Over time, the temple became the center of Jewish worship, with the Holy of Holies—entered only once a year by the high priest—serving as the physical focal point of God's presence on earth. Here was one place where heaven and earth met.

Yet for all the attention given to the building and ritual ceremonies associated with temple worship, the prophets never lost sight of the fact that God could not be reduced to a fixed place or a liturgical formula. The prophet Micah asked,

With what shall I come before the LORD; and bow down before the exalted God? Shall I come before him with burnt offerings, with calves a year old? Will the Lord be pleased with thousands of rams, with ten thousand rivers of oil? Shall I offer my firstborn for my transgression, the fruit of my body for the sin of my soul?

The answer for Micah was clear—what God desires most is a transformed way of living. "He has showed you, O man, what is good. And what does the Lord require of you? To act justly and to love mercy and to walk humbly with your God" (Micah 6:6-8).

The prophet Amos was even more explicit:

I hate, I despise your religious feasts; I cannot stand your assemblies. Even though you bring me burnt offerings and grain offerings, I will not accept them. Though you bring choice fellowship offerings, I will have no regard for them. Away with the noise of your songs! I will not listen to the music of your harps. (Amos 5:21-23)

Instead, Amos thunders, "let justice roll on like a river, righteousness like a never-failing stream!" (verse 24). The worship that God most desires, it would seem, has to do with humble hearts and holy lives committed to justice and righteousness.

Places and Spaces of Christian Worship: From the Early Church to the Reformation

The coming of the Messiah marked both a continuation and a break with these themes. On the one hand, Jesus clearly challenged the Jewish traditions of ritual worship. He openly violated purity laws, for example, by associating publicly with women and by healing on the Sabbath. He bewildered and irritated many of his Jewish listeners by telling them that the temple would be destroyed and then rebuilt in three days—a prophecy that made no sense at all until his own death and resurrection. In a dramatic gesture, Jesus overturned the money-changing tables in the temple, insisting that the building was a house of prayer, not a commercial establishment. At the dramatic conclusion of the crucifixion, the curtain hiding the Holy of Holies in the temple was torn from top to bottom, suggesting that God's Spirit could no longer be confined to a specific place but was unleashed into all the world.

At Pentecost, the Holy Spirit offered further evidence that worship was no longer to be confined to the temple or ceremonial rituals. Yet even here the Spirit was made visible to those present in tangible ways: tongues of fire, blowing winds, the persuasive power of Peter's sermon, and the sudden ability of the disciples to speak in languages that could be understood by people from all over the known world. Moreover, the disciples continued to go to the local synagogue for prayer, they gathered for meals, they shared their possessions, they healed the sick and raised the dead. Although the forms of worship had changed, there was no getting around the material expressions of Spirit's presence.

As the movement grew, so did the hostility of both Jewish leaders and Roman authorities. Increasingly, the early Christians found themselves unwelcome in Jewish synagogues and persecuted by Roman magistrates. Their worship now happened in secret, usually in private homes but sometimes in caves or catacombs.

Not until the fourth century, when persecution ended, did Christians begin to meet in buildings specifically designed for worship. The earliest public churches seem to have been large, rectangular meeting rooms called "basilicas." Basilicas originally served civic and imperial purposes, focusing especially on the worship of the Roman emperor. Christians simply repurposed the space, substituting God for the emperor as the focus of worship and installing an altar in the east end, behind which the bishop presided.

Over time, as the focus of worship shifted increasingly to the celebration of the eucharist, a new design emerged that divided the public space of the basilica into two sections. The larger portion (the nave) was designated for the laity or congregation with the clergy presiding over worship in the sanctuary. By concentrating the focus of worship on the altar and the ritual of communion in the sanctuary, this new design heightened the role of the clergy and introduced a distinction between secular and sacred space. That the entire service was conducted in Latin further underscored a sense of the otherness of God and an awareness that this was a space set apart from the ordinary world.

Church architecture in western Europe took on its most dramatic expression in the twelfth and thirteenth centuries with the emergence of the Gothic cathedral. Towering above the skyline of many European cities, these imposing structures came to embody a fully developed theological worldview. Most cathedrals, for example, were oriented toward the east so that the congregation would be facing Christ when he returned in glory. An arm (or transept) now intersected with the long rectangle of the basilica so that the basic floor plan would take the form of a cross.

Like the Christian church itself, cathedrals were understood to be timeless structures that took generations to build and were intended to last forever. The visionary masons who laid the first foundations also oversaw the cultivation of oak groves that they knew would take at least a century to mature so that timber would be available for later stages of the construction. Villagers hauled the stones piece by piece from quarries that were sometimes miles from the construction site. Master carpenters, stonecutters, and masons spent decades working on a single phase of the project.

When the invention of supporting structures known as "flying buttresses" made it possible to build higher and higher walls, cathedral design began to focus on the luminescent qualities of light. Gradually, stained-glass windows filled the elongated walls, illumining the cathedral with a canvas for telling biblical stories and giving full expression to the divine gift of beauty. The west entrance to the cathedral invited churchgoers to contemplate a complex array of carved stone images that told the church's story in three-dimensional form: depictions of Creation, the fall, Noah's ark, the Exodus, Moses on Mount Sinai; images of the Old Testament kings and prophets; the story of the angel's visit to the Virgin Mary; the birth of Christ; the massacre of the Innocents; representations of the parables of Jesus; scenes from his life, death, and resurrection; images of the apostles and the martyrs of the early church. Overarching it all: a dramatic scene of the return of Christ, Judgment Day, and Christ's triumphant rule over the cosmos itself.

In addition to the altar that dominated the front of the cathedral, architects paid close attention to chapels in alcoves along the sides, to the placement of tombs and mausoleums, and to elaborately carved pulpits. Some cathedrals featured prayer labyrinths embedded in the floor tiles or, in later centuries, highlighted the technological wonders of astronomical clocks and massive pipe organs that flooded the space with music.

Modern visitors today can read into these Gothic cathedrals whatever they wish: an economic statement about the prominence of a town; an assertion of the church's power and authority; a cultural feat of engineering; an aesthetic triumph; or perhaps a symbol of oppression of the peasants whose labor and taxes made it all possible. Medieval theologians were not entirely of one mind about their meaning either. The twelfth-century Cistercian abbot Bernard of Clairvaux worried that the extravagant cathedrals encouraged people to "contribute rather than to pray" and that the sheer grandiosity of the structure made a mockery of the Christian virtues of contrition, penitence, and humility.

At the time of the Reformation, some Protestant groups picked up on these criticisms and condemned cathedrals as idolatrous, wasteful, and promoting bad faith. When these groups moved into Catholic churches, they almost always removed statues of popes, muted the focus on the Virgin Mary, and brought the pulpit into clearer view in an effort to give more attention to the place of Scripture and the sermon in worship. Some groups—especially those in the Reformed tradition—were determined to strip Catholic churches of all their decorative elements, even to the point of destroying statues, altars, and stained-glass windows, and whitewashing the interior of the church. These "purifying" impulses left a deep legacy in Protestant groups like the Baptists and the Pentecostals, who continue to nurture an austere aesthetic evident in the very simple and highly functional church structures scattered in communities across North America today.

Yet anyone who has wandered into a Catholic cathedral and pondered the immensity of space, the layers of theological meaning, the attentiveness to detail, the weight of tradition, and the sheer beauty of the structure cannot help but sense that one is entering a sacred place. Clearly, medieval cathedrals are not the only model of appropriate worship spaces in the Christian tradition. But those in the Anabaptist-Mennonite tradition could learn a great deal about the way worship spaces embody theological convictions by being more attentive to the deeper tradition of church architecture and the formative power of physical space in our worship.

Anabaptist-Mennonite Places and Spaces of Worship

The early Anabaptists, as we have already noted, rejected the Catholic emphasis on visual or material aids to worship as encouraging an unbiblical view of faith. They understood the church to be first and foremost the gathered community, rather than a building. Lavish cathedrals, visual images of saints, and a focus on relics and sacred pilgrimage sites seemed to border on idolatry. Worship, they insisted, is best expressed not in formal rituals controlled by an ordained clergy, but in the lived experience of daily discipleship. These suspicions were reinforced by the hostility of religious officials, who made it impossible for the Anabaptists to worship in public.

It is not surprising, then, that groups in the Anabaptist-Mennonite tradition were very slow to develop a distinctive architectural style for church buildings. In the Netherlands, the government permitted Mennonites in the seventeenth century to construct churches, but only if their exterior facades appeared to be homes or faceless warehouses. The Singelkerk in Amsterdam is probably the most famous example of this "hidden church" (*Schuilkerk*) style. From the outside, the church looks exactly like a three-story residence or apartment house. Past a narrow entrance hallway, however, the interior of the church suddenly opens up into a spacious and beautiful sanctuary, replete with an elevated pulpit, balcony, and pipe organ, and a space capable of seating nearly one thousand people.

Elsewhere in Europe, prohibitions against Mennonite churches relaxed only in the early nineteenth century. At that point, North German Mennonite congregations in urban centers like Crefeld and Hamburg began to construct very large church buildings, generally along the dominant style of their Protestant neighbors, which reflected the elevated income and status of the membership. Also in the nineteenth century, descendents of the Dutch Mennonites who had moved into colonies in south Russia developed a more modest style of church house, modeled on their single-story long barns. Over time, as the colonies became wealthier, these simple Russian Mennonite "prayer houses" (*Bethaus*) evolved into a much more elaborate structure, often constructed out of brick or stone in neo-Gothic style that became full-fledged "churches" (*Kirchen*).

Mennonite worship spaces in Switzerland and South Germany followed a somewhat similar pattern. In Switzerland, persecution lasted through much of the seventeenth century, forcing congregations to meet for worship secretly in private homes, isolated barns, or outdoors. By the eighteenth century, Mennonites who immigrated to the territories of southwest Germany no longer feared active persecution, though the edicts of toleration almost always demanded that they conduct their worship services in private, meeting in homes or in buildings that did not resemble state-approved churches.

When these groups immigrated to the United States in the eighteenth and nineteenth centuries, they were free for the first time to construct church buildings in whatever style they wished. The Amish in North America maintained the older tradition of meeting for worship in homes or barns, a practice that continues to serve them well today. Meeting in houses keeps the primary identity of the congregation rooted in face-to-face relationships as guests or hosts. It also frees congregational resources from being tied to a building that remains largely empty for six days of the week, and it ensures that their congregations remain relatively small. When the group becomes too large to meet in an average home, the congregation divides and creates a new district.

Mennonite churches in North America were initially simple structures, usually dominated by a large, rectangular space with the pulpit located in the center of one of the long sides of the building. The congregation sat facing each other on benches, either divided on both sides of room or arranged on three sides of the rectangular meetinghouse. The interior of a typical Mennonite "meetinghouse" (*Versammlunghaus*) in pre-Civil War United States was very plain, with clear windows to allow for natural sunlight. The simplicity of style suggested a modest aesthetic with a strong emphasis on the church as a gathered community rather than a physical structure.

Here, too, however, as Mennonites became increasingly wealthy and more assimilated into the local community, their church architecture became more varied in style. During the twentieth century, Mennonite congregations built hundreds of new churches, often beginning with the plain meetinghouse style, before slowly incorporating new features, borrowed from the prevailing style of the day, such as steeples, exterior columns, porticos, and even bell towers.

Today it would be difficult to identify most Mennonite churches on the basis of their architecture alone. Although contemporary North American Mennonites have the liberty and resources to design whatever structures they wish for worship, Mennonite church buildings do not always express the distinctive emphases of the Anabaptist-Mennonite tradition.

Contemporary Considerations: Theology, Aesthetics, and Function

Spaces and places of worship are never neutral. Even when we are not aware of it—indeed, perhaps especially when we are not aware of it—our worship spaces are always shaping us and communicating something to the world about who we are and what we believe. Yet if worship is indeed the occasion when we express our deepest understandings of reality and publicly name our highest allegiances, then we should be more attentive to the spaces where that happens.

As Mennonite congregations reflect on the nature of their worship spaces, they would do well to be attentive to three interrelated considerations, asking in each case what insights Scripture and the Anabaptist-Mennonite tradition might have to offer as they make decisions regarding their church buildings. None of these considerations exist fully independent of the others, so distinguishing them is a somewhat artificial exercise. But it might nonetheless be useful to consider them as three distinct voices, each of which must be part of the conversation whenever congregations are considering construction or renovations.

1. The first consideration is theological. Here it is crucial for the congregation to reflect carefully on its fundamental convictions as they find expression in the church's identity and mission: how will these theological commitments be visibly expressed and nurtured in the space they are creating? As we have seen, for Catholics, every aspect of the cathedral is understood to be a response to this question, beginning with the focal point on the altar and the celebration of the eucharist as the central purpose of the worship service. Protestant churches, by contrast, have tended to design their buildings around the pulpit, which is often elevated to occupy a position of clear authority over the members who are seated in straight rows, ready to receive the word. Catholic churches almost always have a cross hanging visibly in the public space of worship, usually with the body of Christ depicted in a way that emphasizes his suffering. Protestant churches also often feature crosses, though they are nearly always empty as a way of focusing on Christ's victory over the power of sin and death.

The distinctive theological themes relevant to Anabaptist-Mennonite congregations cannot be narrowly prescribed. But they might include the following:

- *Seating.* Given the strong emphasis in Anabaptist-Mennonite theology on the church as the gathered community—the body of Christ—Mennonite churches may consider arranging chairs in a semicircle (or the pews on three sides of the worship space) as a way of expressing a central value of the tradition. Some studies have suggested that humans cannot recognize individual faces at distances greater than fifty feet. Sitting in a semicircle allows members of the congregation to easily see each other and to be reminded that our individual relationship to God is inseparable from our relationship to each other. These convictions might also raise doubts about balcony seating in Mennonite congregations. Balconies may allow more people to occupy the worship space, but those seated there will likely experience worship more as spectators rather than full participants.

• *The pulpit.* Even though the sermon remains a central feature of Mennonite worship, the strong emphasis on the priesthood of all believers would suggest that all members share in the responsibility of reading and interpreting Scripture. This means that the Word as it is preached calls for a response; the sermon is not the final word, issued from on high. Thus Mennonite churches may wish to use a lectern rather than an imposing pulpit and to locate it closer to the congregation. Any elevation is primarily for the purpose of being seen and heard rather than as a symbol of authority.

• *Visual witness.* Although we may not often think of it as a theological statement, the exterior design of our churches offers a public witness to our theological values. Regardless of the actual reality, a storefront church, for example, suggests a congregational commitment to be engaged in the life of the neighborhood. A cathedral suggests a church deeply rooted in tradition. A stone church with towers hints at a theology that is fixed, defensive, and unmoving. A megachurch at the edge of town just off the interstate suggests a congregation of busy people looking for a well-packaged program. Whether you intend it or not, the exterior design of your church communicates a set of theological assumptions. Mennonite churches may want to accent themes such as simplicity, integrity, and hospitality.

• *Stewardship of resources.* Just how much money to spend on a church building is a perennial and vexing question. Some people are inclined to argue that just as the children of Israel offered burnt offerings to God, or Mary Magdalene lavished expensive perfume on the feet of Jesus, extravagant expenditures on a church building might be understood as a genuine expression of stewardship—a gesture of truly "letting go" of our possessions. Nothing is too expensive since our intention is to honor God. Others, by contrast, are inclined to think of virtually every penny spent on church buildings as inherently selfish, as money not spent in more worthy causes of missions or charity. For much of their history, Mennonites have been inclined to value frugality in expenditures on church buildings. Many congregations have drawn heavily on the skills and "sweat equity" of their own members in building projects, not only as a cost-saving move but also as a way of building a deeper sense of community. Others have committed to tithing a percentage of money raised for their capital campaigns to support less-wealthy congregations elsewhere. Behind all these questions is the central theme of God's abundance: how will we adequately express our gratitude to God for riches we possess that go far beyond what we actually need?

• *Other considerations.* In addition to some of these basic considerations, congregations making decisions about their worship space should be attentive to a host of other implicit theological statements. How hospitable, for example, is your space to newcomers (clear entrances? signage?). How welcoming is your space to people with physical disabilities (accessible? large print bulletins?

hearing assistance devices?). Most U.S. Mennonite congregations would not prominently display an American flag, recognizing that the body of Christ transcends national identity and borders. Some congregations have intentionally designed their spaces with windows in the front to remind congregants of the connection between worship and our life and witness in the world. What are the theological considerations about having a clock visible in the sanctuary? What kind of artwork or banners will you display in your public spaces? How much more money would you be willing to pay to make your building energy efficient? These are only a few of the many considerations that are reflected in our worship spaces— all of them hinting at theological convictions that are real, even if they are not stated explicitly.

2. The second consideration is the functional *needs of the congregation.* For many Mennonite congregations, functional concerns tend to lead the way in building design, driving many other decisions. And for good reason. Spaces where we gather should serve the practical purposes of our gathering.

How the building accommodates or enables the various aspects of congregational life says a great deal about what the church values. If, for example, you have a worship space that seats three hundred but can accommodate only one hundred fifty for a fellowship meal, you have made a crucial decision about the relative importance of informal gatherings for the life of the church. What kind of kitchen is needed? The amount of space given over to Christian education, youth recreation, and the needs of infants must also be balanced with the space devoted to formal worship. Will you build with a view toward multiple uses? Can your church incorporate other ministries like a nursery or daycare, a food kitchen or homeless shelter, office space for area ministries, or meeting rooms for local organizations? Carpet in the worship area dampens ambient noise during the service, but it also tends to deaden the acoustics of congregational singing. What kind of resources should the congregation invest in a church cemetery? Does the church claim its deceased members as a "cloud of witnesses," or are cemeteries public concerns to be addressed by the state?

Clearly, it is impossible to separate these functional questions from theological questions, since functionality is always a matter of prioritizing according to some sense of value. But thoughtful congregations will be attentive to the full range of practical needs of the congregation and will need to make choices that take these functional concerns into careful consideration.

3. The third, and perhaps most challenging, consideration is **aesthetics.** Deciding what color to paint the hallway may not seem like such a big deal, and you may not personally care about the style of artwork on the walls of the fellowship hall or whether the banners in the sanctuary are purchased from professionals or made by members of the congregation. Yet debates over aesthetic judgments can quickly become very intense precisely because these considerations are so closely linked to individual taste and subjective opinions based on personal likes and dislikes.

Notions about appropriate colors, for example, can reflect simply the mood of the times (during the 1980s, fuchsia and mauve suddenly swept through public spaces across the United States). Some people would not dream of having artificial flowers in the church, while others may find them to be a convenient, inexpensive, and responsible alternative to buying fresh flowers in December, imported from South America. No painting of Christ has been reproduced more often than the famous portrait by Warner Sallman. For some Christians, the painting is a kind of icon; looking at the brown-toned face of Jesus evokes a host of warm feelings about a close relationship with God. Yet for others, the painting seems overly sentimental, a form of kitsch.

Precisely because we are entering a space where we anticipate the world of time and eternity to intersect, our judgments about the aesthetics of worship will evoke a range of opinions. In a healthy congregation, this a very good thing since it prompts us to think more careful about the wonderful, complex range of ideas, experiences, emotions, and convictions that shape our expectations regarding worship.

Aesthetic judgments cannot be reduced to theological arguments of right and wrong, or to pragmatic considerations of function. Some people simply like large, bright, open sanctuaries with vaulted ceilings; others prefer intimate spaces that provide a sense of safety and belonging. At the very least, however, congregations should attempt to define some basic orienting principles and then work very hard to build consensus among those with differing sensibilities.

Artists serving the congregation should be free to exercise their creative gifts. At the same time, they should also be cautious about regarding the spaces of worship as a canvas for individual experimentation, and they should be able to articulate a coherent theological vision of their work. By the same token, just as a good sermon will occasionally surprise, discomfit, and stretch, congregations should be open to the possibility of art or decoration that challenges established assumptions. A visual image of Jesus washing the feet of the world's most powerful people, including Osama bin Laden, may not be a permanent fixture in the church foyer, but making it visible during Lent might serve the congregation well. Perhaps for another season of the year it could be replaced by Sallman's more familiar portrait or by an iconographic representation of Jesus from the Greek Orthodox tradition.

In the end, of course, the spaces in which we worship are not primarily about us, but about how we enter, together, into the presence of God. Here there is ample room for humility and mystery.

Conclusion

Although I was not aware of it at the time, the small Mennonite congregation in central Ohio that I attended as a child had purchased their building from an Evangelical Covenant church. Initially, almost everything in the original structure remained basically intact. The worship space was classically Protestant: a rectangular "box" oriented to two pulpits—the larger one on the left for ordained preachers and the smaller on the right, designated for women and lay speakers. Long, straight, wooden pews focused the attention of worshippers on the front, where a large, red curtain hid the now-unused baptismal font. Elegant stained-glass windows—their muted colors depicting the Lamb of God, a shock of wheat, a symbolic rendering of the Trinity, and even the names of several benefactors—lined both sides of the sanctuary.

Lights hung from above, encased in luminescent iron frames that looked like the turrets of a medieval castle. If you squinted a certain way, the 252 decorative squares on the ceiling would suddenly shift their form and become trapezoids. Built into the wooden pews were small racks with round holes, designed to hold thimble-sized communion cups. On the south wall, opposite the pulpit, a large mural depicted Jesus praying in the garden of Gethsemane. Completed in the early 1930s by a traveling artist named J. Franklin Caveny, the painting was an exact replica of the original completed fifty years earlier by Heinrich Hoffman for the Riverside Church in New York City.

A damp basement provided Sunday school space, and a tiny kitchen quickly overflowed whenever we had fellowship meals. Each Sunday, several men in the congregation arranged long planks down the front steps of the church so that an elderly member, confined to a motorized wheelchair, could enter and exit the building.

In the decades since then, the Mennonite congregation has slowly transformed the building to better reflect its own priorities and convictions. Somewhere along the way, the pulpits and pews were removed, along with the baptismal font. The entire seating arrangement is now reoriented so that the congregation sits in moveable chairs in a semicircle facing a simple lectern and the stained-glass windows along the west wall. A large fellowship space has been added with partitions that can create Sunday school rooms or open into the sanctuary area if additional space is needed for family reunions or wedding receptions. Although the restrooms are still not fully accessible, a ramp has replaced the front steps. The steeple has since disappeared, and a new brick facade with large, glass doors has made the front of the church feel more welcoming. More recently, the trustees installed a remote-controlled screen that can drop down behind the lectern for PowerPoint projection, flanked by two stained-glass windows.

When I return to the church of my childhood, I am struck by the changes. Churches, like the congregations who gather in them, are living things. We shape the spaces that, in turn, shape us. When I visit now as a guest, my thoughts turn not only to the physical space of the church but also to the people in that building who helped to shape my life: a favorite Sunday school teacher; vacation Bible school; friends in my youth group; the elderly pastor who baptized me; a men's group that invited me to participate in a Mennonite Disaster Service assignment.

Sitting in that space also evokes memories that go even deeper. The familiar images depicted in the stained-glass windows, the elegant light fixtures, the Caveny painting of Christ in the garden of Gethsemane—all these tangible objects trigger an awareness that this is a place somehow removed from ordinary time and space, a place where something important is happening. When I witnessed baptisms, foot washing, and communion in that space, when I heard Scriptures read, prayers offered, the doxology sung, and the benediction intoned, I knew even as a child that I was participating in something far bigger than the tiny congregation that had assembled on that Sunday morning.

"What is this place where we are meeting?" Yes, it is indeed "only a house" with walls, a roof, and a floor. But it also is much more than that. At a crucial point in the first verse, the hymn takes a turn. Yes, the church is "only a house." Yet, as the writer of the hymn acknowledges, "it becomes a body that lives when we are gathered here, and know our God is near."[15] In that moment—when the "house" becomes a "body that lives"—we are invited once again to participate in the joyful mystery of the incarnation when the line between worship and witness disappears.

Part 3

Looking Forward

9

Renewing Mennonite Baptism and the Lord's Supper

One beautiful spring morning, our congregation gathered, as we do each year, to celebrate a baptismal service. The event is a highlight of the church year and an important part of our congregational identity. First, we gather in the fellowship hall for breakfast. Then, as the tables are being cleared, someone leads out in the folk hymn "I Went Down to the River to Pray," which we sing with gusto before piling into cars to caravan to a local pond.

As the sun rises, the congregation assembles on blankets and folding chairs for the service. At some point, a member of the church—for youth, it is often a mentor—offers a short introduction and recommendation for each baptismal candidate, followed by a statement of faith and seriousness of intent from the candidates themselves. After the formal baptismal vows, we focus our attention on the dramatic high point of the morning: baptism by immersion and a welcome of the sputtering new member with a white towel and a congregational prayer of blessing. As always, the service is joyful and moving. By the benediction, more than a few of us are pulling out handkerchiefs.

Although the specific details vary widely from church to church, the ritual of baptism is a familiar event in Mennonite congregations. So familiar, in fact, that it seems almost unthinkable that in the sixteenth century this simple act was the source of so much controversy. The issue, of course, was not baptism itself. Virtually everyone in the sixteenth century agreed that baptism—like the Lord's Supper—was a biblical practice that Jesus taught to his disciples and that the early church adopted as an essential Christian ritual. Rather, the debate was over the meaning of baptism and the closely related question of the appropriate age of baptism.

When the Anabaptists began to link baptism with repentance and a conscious decision to follow Jesus—thereby rejecting the long-standing Catholic tradition of infant baptism—authorities responded harshly. It did not help matters that the early Anabaptists also rejected the Catholic mass, challenging the church's long-standing teaching that the bread and wine of communion actually became Christ's body and blood. The Anabaptist challenge to these central points of Catholic doctrine was so threatening that by 1529 the Holy Roman Emperor pronounced the death penalty on anyone caught teaching them. Perhaps as many as three thousand Anabaptists were executed in the course of the sixteenth century for their allegedly heretical teachings.

Modern people find it difficult to understand why these practices were such a big deal. After all, the actions themselves appear to be completely innocent gestures: pouring water, eating a portion of bread, and drinking a sip of wine or grape juice. Yet clearly something deeply significant was at stake. As we shall see, baptism and communion matter so much because they distill the essence of the themes we have been addressing. As worship practices, they capture the moment in worship when heaven and earth meet. They celebrate the reconciliation of humans with God. They are the rituals that give shape to the body of Christ. In short, they are the foundational practices of the church, the point at which worship and witness join together.

In this chapter I want to explore the themes of baptism and the Lord's Supper more closely, first by clarifying more fully why the

Anabaptists rejected the traditional Catholic understanding. Then, and more importantly, I want to note several unintended consequences that have resulted from Mennonite teachings on baptism and the Lord Supper and outline an alternative understanding of "sacraments" based on the thought of an Anabaptist lay theologian named Pilgram Marpeck. Finally, the chapter concludes with a series of suggestions for the Mennonite church to consider regarding these practices in the future.

Clearly, this will not be a full treatment of baptism and the Lord's Supper. But I do hope that anyone interested in a renewal of worship, missions, and Christian discipleship will find here a useful framework for further conversation.

Catholic Understandings of the Sacraments, and the Anabaptist Critique

For nearly a thousand years, the Catholic Church regarded baptism and the Lord's Supper as foundational practices—sacraments—that were crucial to the very identity of the church. Although the word *sacrament* does not actually appear in the Bible, by the early Middle Ages, it had come into common usage as a way of describing a specific expression of God's saving presence in the world. Perhaps the simplest definition comes from Augustine, a fourth-century church father, who defined sacraments as "a visible form of an invisible grace." The visible or material form of a sacrament could refer to various substances: the oil in holy anointing, for example, or the bread of communion or the water in baptism. Used as sacraments, oil, bread, and water were understood to be "signs" that represented God's divine grace. But according to the teaching of the Catholic Church, sacraments are not *merely* signs. That is, they do not merely "represent" divine grace; they actually *bring about* God's grace in the recipient. Medieval theologians sometimes referred to sacraments as "effective signs," signs that actually "effect"—or bring about—the grace of God to which they are pointing (*Signum sacro sanctum efficax gratiae*).

In more specific terms, this meant that the water of baptism was both a sign of God's grace and the necessary means by which God's salvation was conveyed. This was the basis for the Catholic teaching of infant baptism. Since sin, they taught, was inherited at birth, a child should receive the gift of salvation as soon as possible so as to escape the punishment of sin, which was eternity in hell. Thus, when an ordained priest baptized a baby with water immediately after birth, the child's spiritual security was ensured.

In a similar way, when a priest consecrated the bread and the wine of the Lord's Supper, the bread was literally transformed into the body of Christ and the wine into the blood of Christ. Even though the outward appearances remained the same, the essence of the physical substance is transformed in the sacramental act, so that the recipient of communion is no longer ingesting ordinary bread and wine but partaking of the very body of Christ.

For many religious traditions, sacramental rituals—especially the celebration of communion—are the high point of the worship service, the real reason for coming to church on Sunday. Thus, in a typical Catholic mass, there is a sense in which everything associated with the service—Scripture reading, songs, prayers, the priestly vestments, the focus on the altar, the smell of incense, the sound of bells—is preparation for that moment in which the bread and the wine are consecrated. This is how a transcendent, invisible, all-powerful, eternal God is made visible in the world of time and space. This is how the Word becomes flesh. This is the moment in which heaven and earth meet. Once the eucharist has been shared, the service comes to an end and congregants quickly reenter the world of ordinary time.

Clearly, the Anabaptist rejection of infant baptism and the mass was not merely a minor debate over procedures. It challenged the very heart of the Catholic sacramental worldview. Part of the disagreement was a consequence of the growing accessibility to Scripture brought about by the Reformation. Based on their reading of the New Testament, early Anabaptist leaders argued that the Catholic understandings of infant baptism and the Lord's Supper were not grounded in Scripture. In the case of baptism, they noted that Jesus himself was not baptized until the age of thirty. Furthermore, Jesus made it clear in the Great Commission that baptism should be preceded by repentance—"Whoever believes and is baptized will be saved" (Mark 16:16)—something infants cannot do. Peter repeats virtually the same words in his sermon following Pentecost when he called on his listeners to "repent and be baptized . . . for the forgiveness of your sins" (Acts 2:38).

In the Anabaptist understanding, baptism was "an outward sign of an inward transformation." It was a public act that symbolized one's sincere repentance from sin, the entrance into fellowship with the body of Christ, and a readiness to follow Christ in daily discipleship through the power of the Holy Spirit. But baptism itself was only a sign or a symbol. It pointed toward a deeper reality, but it did not, in itself, have any intrinsic spiritual power.

The Anabaptists brought a similar interpretation to the Lord's Supper. They taught that when Christ said, "this is my body . . . this is my blood," his disciples surely understood this to be meant in a figurative way—"this *represents* my body/blood"—rather than literally. When he instructed them to follow his example by eating bread and drinking wine, he did so as a reminder, as a memorial, of his suffering and love ("do this in remembrance of me"). Moreover, both the Bible and later creeds of the church teach that the physical body of Christ ascended into heaven where he is "seated at the right hand of God" until the Last Judgment."[16] Therefore, it was simply not possible for Christ to be physically present in the communion bread and wine every time a church celebrated mass.

The Anabaptists were especially critical of the argument that sacraments actually effected salvation in and of themselves (*ex opere operato*), regardless of the moral qualities of the officiating priest or the attitude of the recipient. In their experience, this promoted a "magical" understanding of church rituals that completely separated divine grace from any concern for moral behavior. How was it that a priest who was known to drink excessively, cavort with prostitutes, and dispute with his neighbors could pronounce the crucial words of consecration at baptism or the Lord's Supper? Equally troubling, how was it that villagers who had been baptized as infants and routinely partook of communion showed no evidence of a transformation of life?

Behind these concerns was a deep resentment of the way in which the church used its authority over the sacraments as a means of controlling its members. Since the sacraments were effective only if an ordained priest officiated, the institutional hierarchy of the church held a monopoly on access to God and the gift of divine grace. Yet Christ had promised to be present "where two or three come together in my name" (Matthew 18:20). The gift of God's grace, the Anabaptists taught, was freely available to anyone who repented of sin and was prepared to walk in the footsteps of Christ.

More than in the water of baptism or the bread and wine of communion, Christ was present in the daily activities of his followers. Wherever the fruit of the Spirit was made visible in the world through practices like mutual aid, hospitality to strangers, or compassion for the enemy, there Christ was present. This was the true sacrament: Christ's divine presence made visible in the life of his followers.

In the centuries since then, relations between Mennonites and Catholics have warmed considerably. Yet memories of persecution still persist among Mennonites, and fundamental differences regarding the sacraments continue to divide.

Today most Mennonites would say that the water of baptism is nothing more than a sign of the candidate's pledge of faith to Christ; the bread and wine of communion are merely a memorial meal, an act of remembrance focusing on Christ's suffering and our call to follow in his way.

Problems with Mennonite Understandings of the Sacraments

The arguments raised by Anabaptists against the sacramental worldview of the medieval Catholic Church were truly revolutionary. They challenged the authority of the Catholic clergy and the institution of the church, they insisted that the gift of grace was inseparable from a transformation of life, and they shifted the focus of worship away from the mass to the life of the gathered community. These under-standings were not lightly considered, and they became formative themes in the emerging Anabaptist-Mennonite church. But because these convictions emerged in a context of such deep conflict and defensiveness, they have also contributed to several persistent prob-lems in the Anabaptist-Mennonite tradition, problems that help to explain some of our current confusion regarding worship, mission, and identity.

Perhaps the most significant confusion in the Anabaptist-Mennonite tradition has to do with our understanding of the Holy Spirit. It is not that Anabaptists were uninterested in the work of the Spirit, but they were deeply skeptical about claims to authority that were based on direct access to the Spirit's power. Moreover, they were intent on giving visible form to the gospel in a life of discipleship and in the disciplined church. Insisting that baptism and communion were merely signs, devoid of any intrinsic spiritual power or author-ity, reflected these concerns.

Yet Christians cannot help but seek the living presence of God in worship, and if Mennonites are told repeatedly that the Spirit is *not* present at the church's most fundamental rituals of baptism and communion—that water and bread are *merely* signs—then they will almost certainly seek the Spirit's presence in other ways. Thus, throughout their history, large numbers of Mennonites have opted to join with various renewal or revivalist groups—the Church of the Brethren, for example, and the Brethren in Christ and the Missionary Church—in a quest for a deeper sense of the Holy Spirit's presence.

These groups have clearly provided an element of the Christian life that has been undervalued in the Anabaptist-Mennonite tradi-tion. But because they also have a very low view of the sacraments, they have not tended to think of the Spirit's presence as being embod-ied in material or tangible ways. As a result, Mennonites drinking from the streams of these renewal movements have almost always adopted more individualistic forms of private devotion, often with an active personal prayer life and emotion-centered spiritual experience.

As a result, an understanding of the lived practices of Christian discipleship or a concern for the visible church as the primary focus of God's work in the world is inevitably diminished. The Spirit is experienced more than it is embodied.

In quite a different way, Anabaptist-Mennonite skepticism about the Spirit's presence in worship has also encouraged among Mennonites a pattern of legalism and a tendency toward church divisions. If God's holy presence is evident *primarily* in the righteous behavior and disciplined practices of the gathered community, it should come as no surprise that Mennonite groups have been vigilant in creating churches "without spot or wrinkle" (Ephesians 5:27 NKJV). In this quest for moral holiness, Mennonites have taken Paul's warning to the church at Corinth not to take communion "in an unworthy manner" (1 Corinthians 11: 27) quite seriously, often turning the Lord's Supper into a tool of discipline and exclusion. All too frequently, Mennonite anxiety about the purity of the church has been the source of contentious debate over the appropriate standard of worthiness. The result has been numerous divisions and deep memories of broken relationships that have sometimes simmered for generations.

Finally, a more modern but equally problematic tendency among Mennonites has been to suggest that the lived actions of the congregation are a substitute for the more formal practices of baptism and communion. The emphasis on the embodied nature of salvation—the generosity expressed, for example, in a barn raising, the hospitality of a fellowship meal, or the support extended to a single mom—is a clear strength of the Anabaptist-Mennonite tradition. In actual practice, however, Mennonites can easily make an idol of their own "good deeds," so that Christ's presence becomes reduced to a set of intentional behaviors or admirable social practices. Thus, for some contemporary Mennonite congregations, a fellowship meal is a substitute for communion, and baptism becomes little more than a celebration of personal choice or a "coming of age" ritual.

Supporting a local food pantry, advocating for immigrants, and creating a childcare program are all worthy activities. Yet to reduce the sacraments of the church to visible expressions of admirable ethical behavior can easily lead to a form of self-worship that is ultimately disconnected from an encounter with the living God. If the identifying practices of the church could be replicated by a good social-service agency, it should come as no surprise that young people would look on worship as being irrelevant. What would be the compelling reason to gather on Sunday morning with its odd language of confession and prayer?

A Second (Anabaptist) Opinion: Pilgram Marpeck's View of the Sacraments

In light of these recurring problems in the Anabaptist-Mennonite tradition, some Mennonites have opted to join groups that have a higher view of the sacraments—the Episcopalians, for example, or the Catholic or Orthodox churches. But others are taking a closer look at some surprisingly rich but unexplored resources available within the Anabaptist-Mennonite tradition itself that offer a more nuanced view of baptism and the Lord's Supper. Here the writings of Pilgram Marpeck, a sixteenth-century lay theologian, are particularly instructive.[17] Marpeck addressed many of these questions quite explicitly and offered a response that took Catholic sacramental thought seriously while remaining authentically Anabaptist.

Marpeck began his career as a civil official in the Catholic mining town of Rattenberg. When Archduke Ferdinand ordered the execution of several Anabaptists in his region, Marpeck decided that he could not participate in the effort to wipe out the movement. Instead, he resigned his office in 1528 and fled to Strasbourg, France, where he found steady work as a civil engineer and a safe haven for conversation with other religious radicals who had also sought refuge there.

In Strasbourg, Marpeck began a long career as an energetic defender of Anabaptist theology, especially in response to the Spiritualists, who rejected outward ceremonies, and to civil authorities who were ready to defend the Christian faith with violence. By 1532, however, Marpeck was forced to flee Strasbourg. After a decade of itinerant leadership, he eventually found employment as the city engineer in Augsburg, where he lived for the last fourteen years of his life in relative peace, even as he continued to support the underground Anabaptist fellowship there.

Although Marpeck had no formal training and was not a highly systematic thinker, he took the classic questions of Christian theology very seriously. In his response to the Spiritualists, who wanted to get rid of all rituals like baptism and the Lord's Supper, he vigorously defended the humanity of Christ and the necessity of ceremonies in the life of the church. On the other hand, in response to the Lutheran focus on "salvation by grace alone," Marpeck insisted that God's gift of grace—the transformation of the inner person—could not be understood or rightly received apart from a transformation of Christian behavior. In conversation with Anabaptist groups whose quest for the pure church had led to legalism and endless disputes, Marpeck repeatedly emphasized the centrality of the Holy Spirit in Christian discipleship.

The key to thinking about God, Marpeck argued, begins with a proper understanding of the incarnation—the wondrous mystery that "Christ became a natural man for natural human beings." As God incarnate—fully human and fully divine—Jesus marked a fundamental break in human history that had consequences for every aspect of Christian faith and practice. Thus the life and teachings, death, and resurrection of Christ were at the center of Marpeck's entire theology.

Like most of his fellow Anabaptists, Marpeck rejected Catholic arguments for the bodily presence of Christ in the eucharist. He did not believe in transubstantiation, the doctrine that the physical properties of the bread and wine changed in communion. But whereas many Anabaptists regarded ceremonies as "outward signs of an inner transformation," Marpeck went further to argue that the water of baptism and the bread and wine of communion were "of one being with the inward reality they represented."[18] In his view, the physical, material elements of water, bread, and wine were *essential* to the Spirit's transformative presence in worship. Because we can know God only through tangible and material forms—seen most dramatically in the humanity of Christ—God continues to be revealed in history in ways that are simultaneously spiritual and material. Indeed, the Spirit cannot be mediated, or made present, *apart from* the material elements. Marpeck thought ceremonies like baptism and the Lord's Supper were the means by which we encounter, participate in, and are transformed by the presence of God.

In developing his understanding of ceremonies, Marpeck drew heavily on the Christian doctrine of the Trinity. Because of Christ's humanity, God is revealed in humble, material substances like water, bread, wine. But when the water, bread, and wine are received with true inward faith—when the Spirit is present in the believer—the ceremony of baptism or communion becomes an external "co-witness" (*Mitzeugnis*) of the Spirit's work. Thus God the Father acts internally in the hearts of humans, through the Holy Spirit, so that the outward elements of the sacraments "are no longer signs but are one essence in Christ." Insofar as these rituals carry on the presence of Christ in the world, participation in them transforms the believers. In baptism and communion we participate in a new reality. "Whoever has the truth in the heart," wrote Marpeck, "the truth which is pointed to and signified by the external sign, for him it is *no sign* at all, but rather one reality with the inner. . . . For that which the Father does, the Son does simultaneously: the Father, as Spirit internally; the Son, as the church, externally."

Marpeck's view of the sacraments was also closely tied to his understanding of Christian ethics and the character of the church. In partaking of the outward elements of communion, for example, believers *participate* in Christ's body. Just as the Word of God, Jesus Christ, became incarnate in human flesh, so the words of God must also become incarnate in physical reality.

This means that communion is indeed a memorial service—a service of remembering. To share in communion is to actively recall the suffering and self-emptying of the human Christ. But because Christ is also spiritually present in the Holy Spirit, this is not merely a symbolic event. Christ's victory over evil in the resurrection and the gift of the Holy Spirit at Pentecost have made possible a new social reality. Through the redemptive activity in Christ in history, those who have become sons and daughters of God receive a new nature and actually participate in this new reality.

At the same time, Marpeck was emphatic that this transformation of Christian life was possible only through the presence and power of the Holy Spirit. He wrote,

> Without the artistry and teaching of the Holy Spirit, who pours out the love, which is God, into the hearts of the faith, and which surpasses all reason and understanding, everything is in vain. The Holy Spirit proceeds from the Father and Son, and He witnesses to the Father and Son in the hearts of all the faithful. He copies and repeats the perfect law of liberty of Christ. The faithful look into this law of liberty in order that they may fervently do what Christ spoke and commanded.

Therefore, as we participate in Christ's "most holy, deified flesh and bone" in communion, through the presence of the Holy Spirit we also are being "re-membered," re-formed into the living body of Christ. The church thus embodies the living Spirit of God. In its worship and in its life together, the church becomes, in Marpeck's words, "the prolongation of the incarnation." It is the living body of Christ.

If Marpeck Is Right, How Might Our Worship Practices Change?

Although my summary of Marpeck's thought on the nature of Christ's presence in the ceremonies of the church is highly simplified, I suspect that many Mennonites will nonetheless find it needlessly complicated and perhaps even threatening. Why bother with this sort of speculation about what exactly is happening at baptism or communion? Isn't this a return to the same "magical" view of the sacraments held by Catholics? What is gained by complicating our understanding of ceremonies with this talk of "presence" and the Holy Spirit?

Ultimately, the answer to these questions can be found only in the lived experiences of those congregations open to engaging these ceremonies in new ways. But in some ways most of this book has been an effort to suggest a range of possible connections between a renewed understanding of Christ's presence in worship and the public witness of the church. For those open to considering these initiatives, I conclude this chapter with a few additional suggestions and words of encouragement.

1. Remembering our baptism. Anabaptists in the sixteenth century likely had good reason to reject an understanding of baptism, performed on infants who had no memory of it, as a "magical" ritual that somehow, in and of itself, granted salvation. But in defining baptism as merely a sign or as "just" a symbol, Mennonites today risk turning baptism into little more than a routine rite of passage, the significance of which quickly fades from view in the years following. Thus, we are often not particularly troubled if a young person baptized as a teenager quits attending church as a young adult—after all, baptism is "merely" a symbol.

Marpeck's view of the sacraments suggests that it would be more appropriate for us to think of baptism as analogous to marriage. When a man and a women publicly declare their vows to each other before God and the congregation, they are not offering merely a sign of their love. Instead, wedding vows are a performative act that changes reality itself. Obviously, the vow alone does not make a marriage. But the vow changes the couple's status and identity in a real way. Their individual identities have not been erased, but they leave the church with a fundamentally different identity. Their relationship to the larger community has changed too. In a sense, the community itself has been reconfigured by their new relational status. A husband and wife no longer participate in society as two single individuals but as a married couple.

The Mennonite church would do well to bring the same level of seriousness to baptism that we do to marriage. In our baptism we have not merely been splashed with water or participated in a "sweet sixteen" party to announce our entrance into the world of adults.

Baptismal vows, like marriage, change our identity before God and the congregation. In baptism, we have been marked by the cross and claimed by Christ. We have been "tattooed" by our baptism in a way that fundamentally transforms our identity.

It is not that the waters of baptism prompt some sort of mystical spiritual switch to get flipped from hell to heaven. But we do believe that baptism bears visible, tangible witness to the fact that the Holy Spirit is actively at work making us into "a new creation" (2 Corinthians 5:17). A crucial part of this work is our incorporation into the body of Christ—the church. Just as marriage does not eliminate one's personal identity, we enter the church with a host of unique ideas, talents, eccentricities, and problems. But baptism breaks down the old divisions of ethnicity, class, education, gender, race that are so deeply entrenched in our sinful, fallen world. It transforms our identity. In Christ, we who were once divided are now joined together (see Galatians 3:27-28), made into "one new humanity" (Ephesians 2:15 NRSV).

Like marriage, baptism in the Anabaptist understanding is not an assertion of individual rights, but a public statement of allegiance, a profession of loyalty to Christ and the church. To be sure, we enter the journey of faith at different levels of maturity and with varying understandings of what it means to participate in the gathered community. But baptism is nonetheless a binding commitment to each other and to Christ, sealed by the presence of the Holy Spirit.

Therefore, just as we would express concern if a person in our congregation would walk out on his or her marriage, so too we should react quickly and pastorally if a baptized member would unilaterally quit attending church. Unfortunately, however, this is precisely what has been happening among so many of our young people. Although they were baptized into the church in their teenage years, we often are loathe to express any alarm—indeed, some even regard it as a normal stage in spiritual development—if they no longer attend church as young adults. Yet if baptism is a public witness to the presence of Christ incarnated in the world, then we should regard baptized members who are absent from congregational life with the same urgency and pastoral concern that we would bring to members who are contemplating divorce. Such a gesture is not punitive or intrusive but simply a caring response that emerges from the conviction that Christian discipleship is unimaginable apart from the gathered body of Christ.

We also need to be more vigilant about "remembering our baptisms." If baptism is not just a symbol but a public response to God's invitation—marked by the transforming presence of the Holy Spirit, a commitment to walk in the way of Jesus, and our incorporation into the body of Christ—then we should be much more conscious about recalling and renewing its meaning regularly.

On this point I have learned a great deal from my involvement in ecumenical conversations with representatives of the Lutheran church. Although we have fundamental differences regarding the baptism of infants, I have been impressed by one aspect of Lutheran baptismal theology. At some point in virtually every worship service I have attended, someone pours water from a pitcher into a basin while offering an encouragement to "remember your baptism." Most Lutheran churches also have a receptacle with water just inside the entrance so that worshippers can dip their finger into the water—not because the water is holy, as I used to think, but as a conscious gesture of remembering baptism. Woven into the Lutheran liturgy are frequent reminders that our baptism into Christ is for life and needs to be continually called to our attention.

The irony for me as a Mennonite is that, unlike most of my Lutheran friends, I actually can remember my baptism. Yet I hardly ever am encouraged to do so. Remembering our baptism serves as a kind of reset button and calls us to a fresh perspective on our most basic allegiances.

We are forgetful people. If marriages are commemorated on at least an annual basis, with larger public celebrations on key anniversaries, then it certainly would seem appropriate for the church to be much more attentive to remembering and celebrating the baptisms of its members. Being more intentional about remembering our baptism will not in itself turn around the exodus of baptized members from our congregations. But participation in Christ, and in the body of Christ, is a lifelong event in need of continual renewing. Remembering our baptisms may help at least some of us to renew our commitments and awaken a fresh sense of God's presence in our lives.

2. Celebrate communion more frequently. This call to be more deliberate about remembering our baptism raises similar questions about the frequency of communion in our worship. In contrast to many traditions that celebrate communion daily, weekly, or monthly, Mennonites generally observe communion much more infrequently. During the late seventeenth century, Mennonite congregations in Switzerland held communion once a year, usually at Easter. Today, many Mennonite congregations celebrate communion twice a year, often in the spring and the fall, while some groups observe it quarterly.

The rationale for less-frequent practice varies. Some have argued that communion takes away too much time from the sermon or that it makes newcomers uncomfortable. Sometimes Mennonites express concern that more-frequent communion is likely to make the practice feel mechanistic and overly routine. The most theologically coherent argument for entering cautiously into communion comes from Paul's warning to the Corinthians that they not take communion "in an unworthy manner," by which he meant celebrating the unity of the body in communion when there was open dissent in the congregation (see 1 Corinthians 11:27-29). Thus many Mennonite congregations once preceded communion with a series of preparatory practices that included an affirmation by every baptized member of the congregation that they were "at peace" with God and with the members of the church. If anyone was not at peace, communion was postponed until the matter was resolved.

In my judgment, none of these reasons defending infrequent communion seem compelling. Of course there is always a possibility that a ritual action will become routine. But think of all the other routine practices for which the same thing might be said—prayer before a meal, for example, or greeting each other with a handshake, or reminding our children to say thank you. All of these are repetitive gestures. But we recognize that their meaning and importance goes beyond our own personal mental or emotional state when we participate in them. Moreover, these gestures are formative practices that shape us, in part, precisely through their sheer repetition. Eventually, we hope, children who are regularly reminded to say thank you will come to develop a disposition of gratitude toward other people, recognizing that they are indeed blessed by gifts large and small.

The most serious argument against frequent communion—that we not take communion unworthily—applies to Mennonite congregations only if they are actually taking the unity of the body seriously enough to discern whether or not the congregation is indeed at peace, and if they are prepared to withhold communion from members who are not reconciled with each other.

The Lord's Supper is a meal of remembrance, not only in the obvious sense that we are tempted to forget our most basic identity and our truest allegiances, but also in the sense of "re-membering" or restoring a body that has been broken. Communion is a ritual that restores to wholeness that which is separated and divided. As in baptism, those who partake of the Lord's Supper participate in the cruciform nature of Christ's body. And, as in baptism, we are caught up in the resurrection as well—the *real* presence of Christ. Through the presence of the Spirit, we can participate in the living body of Christ and can claim, with the apostle Paul, that "now in Christ Jesus you who once were far off have been brought near by the blood of Christ. . . . Consequently, you are no longer foreigners and aliens, but fellow citizens with God's people and members of God's household" (Ephesians 2:13, 19). Through God's grace, we are truly re-membered in communion as participants with God in the task of making creation whole.

We are forgetful people. Because the modern world is so full of distractions and because we are inclined to worship ourselves or the things we create, we need the regular practice of the Lord's Supper. If worship expresses our deepest understanding of the way the world works and if we think the incarnation is central to our faith, it would seem obvious that we celebrate this central conviction in a more regular and visible way in our worship.

The Lord's Supper calls us to remember who we are in relation to God, and it re-members us as a community bearing witness to be the living body of Christ in the world.

◆ ◆ ◆

Beyond a more conscious commitment to remembering our baptism and incorporating communion more frequently into our worship services, Mennonite congregations will be renewed if they simply nurture practices that cultivate a greater attentiveness to the profound and joyful mystery of the incarnation in *every* aspect of the Christian life. Yes, Christ is present in a unique way at baptism and communion, but the living presence of Christ is not confined to these ceremonies.

As we have seen, the theme of God's presence made visible in the world runs from the Creation story in Genesis to the return of Christ anticipated in Revelation. Because God created the world in Christ and is redeeming it in and through Christ, creation matters. This suggests that all of life is a window into the divine. Christ is the one in whom and through whom all things were created and "in him all things hold together" (Colossians 1:17).

To see the world incarnationally is to see it latent with the Spirit of God. It is to walk gently in the world, anticipating the surprising presence of God. It is to "pray without ceasing" in the awareness of the fundamental blessedness of the world and the underlying coherence of all things, even amid the world's brokenness and pain.

This is salvation! If a secular perspective refuses to see the world and its life as anything other than material, Christians gaze on the world as a sacramental place made by God, transformed by Christ, and being renewed into a new creation through the presence of the Holy Spirit.

Conclusion

Before his ascension, Christ promised his followers that he would not leave them alone: "I am with you always, to the very end of the age" (Matthew 28:20).

In the last chapter of Luke, we read the story of two followers of Jesus returning home from the crucifixion. Cleopas and his friend had been among those who recognized Jesus as the one sent from God. They had seen his miracles, been moved by his teachings, witnessed his triumphal entry into Jerusalem. Here, at last, was the Messiah, the one who would deliver them from oppression under the Romans and usher in the restoration of a new kingdom.

But in the terrible days that followed, their hopes had been cruelly dashed. They had looked on helplessly as Jesus was arrested, given a sham trial, and condemned to be executed. The man who had calmed storms at his command, restored withered limbs to full strength, and brought back the dead to life had been hung up naked on a cross and left to die a slow, painful, and humiliating death. Now, discouraged and sad, they walked along a dusty road back to their home town of Emmaus.

Along the way a stranger joined them. In their conversation, they poured out their story of disappointment and woe. They told the stranger how this prophet, Jesus of Nazareth, "the one who was going to redeem Israel," had been sentenced to death and crucified (Luke 24:21). But then the stranger corrected them. They had not gotten the story straight. Moving through the writings of Moses and the prophets, he reminded them that the Messiah would have to first "suffer these things." Only then could he "enter his glory" (24:26).

When they arrived at the village, Cleopas and his friend persuaded the stranger to join them for a meal before he continued on his way. There, as they gathered around the table, the stranger took bread, gave thanks, broke it, and began to share it with them. Suddenly "their eyes were opened and they recognized him" (24:31). Jesus, the resurrected Messiah, was present at their table! Immediately, Christ vanished. But Cleopas and his companion quickly began to spread the word.

In baptism and communion Christ assured his followers that he would be present with them. Although Christians have stretched their vocabulary to the breaking point in trying to describe the exact nature of Christ's presence in these ceremonies, the promise of Christ is nonetheless as real today as it was two thousand years ago. Perhaps the biggest challenge for believers is not formulating precise theological language; it is praying for the gift of grace to recognize Christ's presence in the humble realities of daily life.

Perhaps our need is not for clearer definitions but, like Cleopas, for the gift of sight.

10

Looking Forward

An Invitation to the 'Beauty of Holiness'

You shall love the Lord your God. . . . Why? . . . [Because]
God, whose face has shone in the face of Jesus Christ, is
supremely beautiful. It is central to Christianity that there is
a resemblance, a relationship, between the beauty we expe-
rience in nature, in the arts, in a genuinely good person and
in God; and that which tantalizes, beckons and calls us in
beauty has its origin in God.

—RICHARD HARRIES[19]

On a bone-chilling evening three days before Christmas 1990, my twenty-four-year-old brother, Steve, died in our family home. For the previous nine months he had engaged in a fierce struggle with cancer, undergoing several rounds of intense chemotherapy, two major operations, and a variety of alternative therapies. By the time the disease spread to his bones, causing relentless and excruciating pain, death came as almost a relief.

The church was packed as we gathered shortly after Christmas for a service of lament and thanksgiving. For several brief hours, we prayed together, sang many hymns, heard words of comfort and consolation from Scripture, expressed our firm hope in eternal life, and then went out into the bitter cold to commit his body to the earth.

That funeral was a distant memory nearly two decades later when a man approached me one evening at a speaking engagement far from home. Hesitantly, he mentioned Steve's name and asked whether I might be related to him. He had seen my last name in an advertisement for the event and had come to the meeting in the off chance that I might be a relative. When I quickly confirmed the connection, he told me his story.

Eighteen years earlier he had worked at the medical school hospital where my brother was being treated. He had been impressed by Steve's reflective response to the illness and intrigued by the steady, supportive presence of friends and family who shared in his pain. Steve lived at home for the last weeks before his death, but the man continued to think about him. When he heard of Steve's death, he tracked down the details and drove two hours to attend the funeral. What happened stunned him.

"I had never been to a funeral, where the words of pain and hope rang so true," he told me, "where the singing was so heartfelt. I can hear it even now. That funeral," he said, now with tears in his eyes, searching for the right words, "that funeral was beautiful!" It changed his life. He returned home, began attending a church, and embarked on a journey of spiritual growth that still continues.

It is not often that we hear the word *beautiful* in association with a funeral. In modern culture, beauty is so closely tied to the fashion industry that the word almost always triggers images of young, healthy, perfectly proportioned bodies wearing the latest fashions. Beauty in popular usage usually means something like "pretty" or "nice." Scientists who have studied human perceptions of beauty focus on qualities like symmetry or hip-to-waist ratios. But beauty itself seems as difficult to explain as the changing whims of fashion. If pressed to define it more precisely, most people are quick to throw up their hands and insist that beauty is subjective and personal. Beauty, we say, is in the eye of the beholder.

But the human hunger for beauty is undeniable. We have all witnessed the ugliness of life. We wince at the pervasiveness of cheap imitations, veneers, and facades. We sense that "true" beauty runs deeper than the surface appearances of a well-proportioned face or body. And we yearn for encounters with beauty that surprise and move us.

Since the time of the ancient Greeks, some philosophers have insisted that beauty is a formal quality, ultimately indistinguishable from goodness and truth. A moral life (goodness) will inevitably be a life of integrity (truth). Wherever morality and integrity join together, beauty will also be present. Beauty cannot coexist with immorality; nor can beauty abide deceit.

Although the Catholic tradition has not generally regarded beauty as a central theological theme, the church nonetheless embraced visual art as a worthy expression of praise to God. Virtually all the architecture, sculpture, and paintings of the Middle Ages were sponsored by representatives of the church who hoped thereby to bring glory to God (and perhaps also to their city). No one can wander through the Gothic cathedral at Chartres or spend an afternoon in the Vatican without recognizing that the architects, sculptors, stonemasons, glassmakers, artists, and artisans who created the rich array of medieval religious art had a deep appreciation for beauty.

Understandings of beauty in the Anabaptist-Mennonite tradition, by contrast, have been more complicated. On the one hand, anyone who has witnessed the geometrically arranged shocks of wheat in a Amish field on a sun-drenched fall day, or stood outside a white, austere Mennonite meetinghouse framed against the backdrop of a neatly ordered cemetery, or seen the exuberant profusion of colors in a flower garden beside an Amish home, or contemplated the majestic array of mason jars laden with tomato juice, green beans, mixed pickle, and applesauce neatly aligned in a fruit cellar knows that beauty is not absent from the tradition. But the moment one presses the question any harder, the topic of beauty immediately becomes problematic.

In its most benign form, Mennonites have traditionally regarded art as unnecessary, frivolous, and maybe even wasteful. The parable of the woman washing Jesus' feet with expensive perfume has always baffled Mennonite preachers. At a somewhat deeper level, the Anabaptist-

Mennonite tradition has nurtured a suspicion about the potential deceit inherent in visual images, where surface appearances capture our attention but are ultimately something other than what they appear to be. A painting, after all, is an illusion, and a play only pretends to be reality. Christians are not called to gaze on the world as an illusion but to participate in it fully as disciples of Jesus. Moreover, skill at creating these artifices often leads to pride.

As a result of these and other concerns, those in the Anabaptist-Mennonite tradition have a somewhat impoverished vocabulary for talking about beauty. Yet just as renewal within the Mennonite church may call for a more sacramental understanding of baptism and the Lord's Supper, so too a renewed understanding of mission in the Mennonite church will need to open itself more consciously to God's presence in the form of beauty. Why? Because beauty is the inevitable consequence of true worship, and because the Christian witness to the world is true only if it is genuinely beautiful.

The Beauty of Holiness

Like humility or goodness, beauty is fundamental to the Christian life. It is not an add-on or an extra or a frill. Yet beauty always resists formal definitions. Although it is real—not merely a figment of our imagination—it can be described only obliquely, from an angle, and by appealing to lots of illustrations.

For the Christian, beauty begins with a recognition of God's deep love for the created world, a love that is embodied in specific ways, even as it exceeds our ability to fully grasp or define. Like the carefully chosen words of a well-crafted poem, beauty is always expressed in the particular. Yet just as the meaning of a carefully wrought poem moves through and beyond the individual words that give it shape, beauty always exceeds its form.

Beauty is revealed in the gift of Jesus, God's self-giving act of love poured out abundantly for the world. When Christians participate in that vulnerable self-opening love, our lives are transformed. Beauty becomes a cup that runneth over. It finds expression in the plenitude of God, who loves into existence beings whom God does not need and who deigns to remain at the disposal of these finite creatures. Beauty is the outpouring of a grateful heart that loves because it receives what it has not deserved.

Beauty is the result of God making heaven and earth from the chaos of the void, of the random, chaotic and formless taking on form. Beauty does not shrink back from the reality of evil or suffering. It is not an escape from pain and grief and sorrow. It is a deep, reconciling embrace of all that is broken and torn asunder in our world. In the words of Eugene Peterson, beauty "names the gathering together of the shards and splinters of broken lives and smashed souls; it is the trace left behind of a patient 'entering into' the mess of chaos and bringing together a new creation that leaves nothing out." Whereas the human impulse to impose order on the world can easily become tyrannical, the beauty of God's order is always an expression of love, made evident in a *rightly ordered* world. This is the beauty of erotic passion within a marriage covenant of abiding trust and fidelity, or the effortless grace of a ballet dancer, whose seeming weightlessness is possibly only through of hours of disciplined practice and a deep attentiveness to form. Contrary to the assumptions of many worship planners, beauty resists the cult of the new. It is precisely in the ordered repetition of our worship practices—the disciplined pattern of the routine—that the slow revelation of beauty finds expression.

Beauty is the evidence of the inherent wholeness of God, often revealed patiently, over time. Late in November 1919, a roving band of anarchists descended on the South Russian Mennonite village of Eichenfeld. In one bloody night, the anarchists executed virtually all the men in the village. Several days later the survivors of the massacre gathered in a circle around a mass grave containing the bodies of all eighty victims. Breaking the stunned silence of the wintry morning, a solitary voice began to sing the familiar hymn by Schubert, "Holy, Holy, Holy." Soon the rest of the villagers joined in harmony, raising their voices together in agony, grief, and praise to God.

Holy, holy, holy, holy is the Lord!
Holy, holy, holy, holy is He alone!
God, who had no beginning,
God, who always was;
Eternally exalted, reigns forevermore
Almighty, wonder, omnipresent love!
Holy, holy, holy, holy is the Lord!

It may seem offensive to speak of beauty in association with heart-wrenching grief and a mass grave. There is nothing beautiful about death—especially violent, mass death that leaves so many widows and fatherless in its wake. Yet I can never hear this hymn or sing it without having an image of the villagers of Eichenfeld raising their voices together. And I am overcome with a sense of beauty.

Beauty is rooted, finally, in the cross itself, where Christ bore our sin and transformed it into the raw material of salvation. I think here of a well-known picture of Mother Teresa. By itself, the photo depicts little more than an aged women with deeply wrinkled skin. A white headscarf with blue stripes offers a sharp contrast to the sad, brown eyes set deep in her weather-beaten face. By standard measures, this image does not meet the criteria for beauty. Yet as your eye lingers on the image, a picture slowly forms of a life of compassion lived in worship to God. Instead of seeing an elderly woman, one begins to see a commitment to caring for the poorest of the poor in the ugliest of circumstances, surrounded by poverty, disease, and death. Slowly you realize that the image is beautiful. This is the *beauty of holiness*.

Sometimes Mennonites have pursued holiness so tenaciously that we have turned it into something quite ugly. In our quest to be holy, we have been tempted to make the church a defensive retreat— a contamination-free zone, cordoned off from the world. By the same token, we have sometimes reacted so strongly against the legalism of the past that we become reeds blowing in the wind in a never-ending quest to be "relevant." If the quest for holiness can become ugly, so too can the urge to accommodate the gospel to the comfortable logic of the culture so that we might avoid the embarrassing paradox of the incarnation. The result is something banal and trivial.

The beauty of holiness does not call us to condemn sinners or to stand around as spectators of the sins and troubles of others. Nor does it suggest that we ignore sin or smooth the edges off the radical claims of Jesus in order to avoid giving offense. Instead, the beauty of holiness calls us to bear the sins of others as an act of intercession, to become fellow sufferers and participants in the sacrificial life of Jesus as he takes on himself the sins of the world.

The beauty of holiness is grounded in love and will inevitably find expression in relationships. It will be active and engaged, not with the explicit goal of fixing every problem in the world but in bearing witness to the deep movement of God's Spirit, who is at work healing creation, even when we do not see it. Beauty emerges in the awareness that God—not us—determines the outcome of history and that, in the fullness of time, history is moving toward the restoration of the whole world, when we will be resurrected in a new body and will join with all creation in a new heaven and a new earth.

What this suggests is that beauty is the true foundation of Christian witness. Unlike so many other tempting approaches to mission, the beauty of holiness uses no gimmicks, makes no guarantees about health or wealth, and issues no threats—real or implied. Instead, beauty is inherently noncoercive and nonmanipulative. The beauty of holiness is like a fragrance that enters into a space and gently, persistently calls attention to itself. It invites, it bears witness, it offers a testimony, but it does not compel or impose. In the end, beauty does not explain or defend or argue for anything. It simply reveals what is already implicit in every detail of creation, what has been there all along.

This is the marriage of worship and witness. This is the beauty of the incarnation—the body of Christ poured out for the world. This is the beauty of holiness.

Conclusion

In this book, I have tried to name some of the sources of the confusion and anxiety evident in the church today as it faces an uncertain future. At the heart of our malaise is an ancient story of separation and division. We are fragmented people, living lives divided from ourselves, from each other, from creation, and, most profoundly, from God. Yet the good news of salvation is that God has not given up on humanity. The creation that God pronounced good yearns to be restored to its intended purpose. In Jesus Christ, God entered fully into human history: the Word became flesh so that we might be restored to the wholeness of body and spirit for which God designed us. In worship, we join our bodies, minds, and hearts in praise to God, practicing the habits of a fully integrated life.

Because we are embodied souls, worship will always be expressed in concrete acts of witness. This is what it means to participate in Christ and to bear fruit as branches of the one true Vine.

Because we are also ensouled bodies, Christian ethics will always be a form of worship. The gift given always exceeds our grasp; it can never be reduced to our hard work or good efforts.

In the Sermon on the Mount, Jesus offered his disciples a summary of the essence of Christian faith. For those in the Anabaptist-Mennonite tradition, the Sermon on the Mount has often been claimed as a kind of shorthand for Anabaptist ethics: here we find the central themes about loving enemies, practicing generosity, and living simply. But it is surely no accident that in the middle of this call to radical discipleship, Jesus offered his disciples instructions on worship, specifically, a model for how they should pray.

The Lord's Prayer is probably the most familiar prayer in the entire Christian church. Millions of Christians know it by memory, and many congregations recite it every Sunday. Indeed, the prayer has become so familiar that we can easily forget just how radical it actually is.

When Christians pray, "Thy Kingdom come, thy will be done, on earth as it is in heaven," we are making an audacious request that should leave us a little bit awestruck. In our daily prayer that "God's kingdom will come, that God's will be done, on earth as it is in heaven" we express our own deep yearning that the brokenness we experience in our families, congregations, communities, and world might be healed. What a revolutionary claim! Christians actually believe that God desires to be reconciled with humanity, that God wants the health and harmony and wholeness of God's original design to be made real and visible on earth, so that we might be reconciled again with God.

When that happens we participate, if only for a moment, in the beauty of holiness.

May our churches be renewed in body and spirit through the power of the incarnation, and may you experience the presence of God "on earth as it is in heaven."

◆ ◆ ◆

A Coda

I wish I could report that since my ill-fated hike on the Appalachian Trail everything has now been resolved—that the practices of worship have laid to rest my spiritual doubts and that the larger church is well on its way to resolving its own conflicted understandings of worship and missions. The truth, not surprisingly, is more complicated than that. As readers of this book will realize by now, my thought and practice are still evolving. This is a travel report of a pilgrim on the way rather than the pronouncements of a fully mature Christian who has finally arrived.

Yet I can say that in the time since that confused attempt to "become spiritual," God's abundance has been revealed to me in some wonderful ways. I have a new appreciation for the value of setting aside time each day for Scripture reading and prayer. I have deeper love for the members of my small group and the gift of a weekly meal and conversation they share with me. I have a new hunger to celebrate communion and am emboldened to speak more freely with students about the claim that the body of Christ has on their lives by virtue of their baptism. I have been richly blessed by lively conversations with Christians from outside the Anabaptist-Mennonite tradition. I have come to think of my faith as participating in and with Christ in a world brimming with evidence of God's presence. I pray every day for the gift of seeing God at work in the world and for a spirit yielded more fully to the Holy Spirit so that my life, and the life of my congregation, might embody the beauty of holiness.

In short, I am more certain than ever that life is a blessing: taste and see that the Lord is good!

Notes

1. Irenaeus, *Against Heresies*, bk. 5, preface.

2. M[aster] Elias Schad, "True Account of an Anabaptist Meeting at Night in a Forest and a Debate Held There With Them," *Mennonite Quarterly Review* 58 (July 1984), 292-95.

3. Theodor Sippell, ed. "The Confession of the Swiss Brethren in Hesse, 1578," *Mennonite Quarterly Review* 23 (January 1949), 22-34.

4 N. T. Wright, "Mere Mission," *Christianity Today*, January 2007, 41.

5. See, for example, the cases cited by Wolfgang Schäufele, "The Missionary Vision and Activity of the Anabaptist Laity," *The Mennonite Quarterly Review* (January 1962), 99-115, and Franklin Littell, "The Anabaptist Theology of Mission," in *Anabaptism and Mission*, ed. Wilbert Shenk (Scottdale, PA: Herald Press, 1984), 18-23.

6. Wendell Berry, "Christianity and The Survival of Creation," *Cross Currents*, 43:2 (Summer 1993), 157.

7. Thieleman J. van Braght, *The Bloody Theater or Martyrs Mirror*, trans. Joseph Sohm, 5th ed. (Scottdale, PA: Herald Press, 1950), 453.

8. The story is recounted in full in Harvey Hostetler, *Descendants of Jacob Hochstetler* (Elgin, IL: Harvey Hostetler, 1912), 26-45.

9. Bryan Stone, *Evangelism After Christendom* (Grand Rapids, MI: Brazos, 2007), 12.

10. Details of this story can be followed best in *Hans Landis: Swiss Anabaptist Martyr in Seventeenth Century Documents*, trans. and ed. James Lowry (Millersburg, OH: Ohio Amish Library, 2003).

11. For the stories that follow, and many additional examples, see Ernst Müller, *Geschichte der bernischen Täufer* (Frauenfeld, 1895),

105-31 and Cornelius Bergmann, *Die Täuferbewegung im Kanton Zürich bis 1660* (Leipzig: M. Heinsius Nachfolger, 1916), 68-102.

12. Georg Thormann, *Probier-Stein oder Schriftmässige und aus dem wahren innerlichen Christenthumb Hergenommene Gewissenhafte Prüfung des Täuffertums* (1693).

13. C. Arnold Snyder, *Anabaptist History and Theology: An Introduction* (Kitchener, ON: Pandora Press, 2005), 106-7. For more on Nadler's remarkable system, see Russell Snyder-Penner, "Hans Nadler's Oral Exposition of the Lord's Prayer," *Mennonite Quarterly Review* 65 (October 1991), 393-406.

14. "What is this place," in *Hymnal: A Worship Book* (Elgin, IL: Brethren Press, 1992), 1.

15. From "What is this place," in *Hymnal: A Worship Book.*

16. See Luke 22:69. This same theme is echoed in the Apostles' Creed, the Nicene Creed and the Athanasian Creed.

17. The biographical and theological information on Marpeck that follows can traced best in the following books: Walter Klaassen and William Klassen, *Marpeck: A Life of Dissent and Community* (Scottdale, PA: Herald Press, 2008); Neal Blough, *Christ in Our Midst: Incarnation, Church and Discipleship in the Theology of Pilgram Marpeck* (Kitchener, ON: Pandora Press, 2007); and John Rempel, *The Lord's Supper in Anabaptism* (Scottdale, PA: Herald Press, 2003).

18. Rempel, *The Lord's Supper in Anabaptism*, 97.

19. Richard Harries, *Art and the Beauty of God: A Christian Understanding*, 2nd ed. (London: Continuum International, 2000), 6.

The Author

John D. Roth is professor of history at Goshen College, where he also serves as director of the Mennonite Historical Library and editor of *The Mennonite Quarterly Review*. He has edited and authored several books, including *Beliefs: Mennonite Faith and Practice; Stories: How Mennonites Came to Be* (companion titles to this book); *A Companion to Anabaptism and Spiritualism, 1521-1700;* and *Engaging Anabaptism: Conversations with a Radical Tradition.*

DATE DUE